MW00777519

craving love

A Girlfriend's Guide

Out of Divorce Hell

into Heaven

and a New Life You Love

Shelly Young Modes

Cover Design: John Matthews, Bluebullseye.com

Editing: Ginger Moran & Kate Makled

Cover Photo Courtesy:
Tina Falkenbury Depicting Life Photography

To All the Believers,
but especially to my Mom and my RLL.

Table of Contents

"There is a kingdom of love waiting to be reclaimed. I am the hunter of invisible game."
– Bruce Springsteen

Preface

"I don't want to talk about them anymore. I don't want to pick apart, analyze, try and figure out my ex husband, my parents, or him, and why things are the way they are anymore. What they did to contribute to where I am now. The situations that we are in now. I don't even want to talk about the situations anymore. I want to fix me. Where is my one last broken piece? What is my part? Where is the place my heart stops and why? What is the last barrier? I want to break it down. I want to love in the purest way. A heart wide open. Where is it I shut down and why, so I can stop? What am I not doing, giving too much of, too little of, withholding, allowing in my own life? Why do I attract what I attract?" I pulled more tissues from the box. "This has to stop, I don't want to do this anymore."

By "this," I meant, this sitting on the couch, talking about the last vestige of my heart, sometimes crying and sometimes not and wondering, why I didn't have what I wanted. All the way.

"What am I doing to keep it from coming?" Her eyes grew large. Her face changed. I'd struck a chord. I am sitting on my friend's sofa, straight from the therapist's office, because I didn't get deep enough into my own heart in the 50 minutes I'd just spent with my therapist. I needed to unravel some more.

"What is preventing me from giving my whole heart? From saying what my heart wants? Why am I hiding that one part of my heart? I've learned enough to know it's me. I speak on this subject, I coach on this subject, I write on this subject. Relationships, attraction, communication, Love. A tiny piece of my truth has eluded me. I know that like attracts like and if I am attracting "emotional unavailability" then there is a part of me that is emotionally unavailable. I must figure it out. Because there is a scenario I want, and when I am asked, I don't want to be afraid to say that's what I want. I don't want to feel like this again. I don't want to be here, in this moment again. I need to figure *me* out. The rest of the way. "This makes me sick," I said. "I feel like such a dumbass."

This is where I am. In the middle of an emotional "perfect storm." A trifecta of grief, wondering, "what just happened here – and why?" My heart has been broken wide open. The term I used with the therapist and my closest confidant is "emotional rock bottom." Both of my parents have died in the last four months. My mom passed away peacefully but quickly in April, after a long and heroic battle with cancer. My dad died only three months later after a tragic motorcycle accident, which resulted in a trauma ICU stay that lasted for two weeks before he also peacefully gave up the will to live. And "the man" in my life and I have walked away from each other, a couple of weeks after my father's death, right about the time one would think one needed that kind of anchor most. After people began questioning the confines of our relationship, when things got dramatic, bigger, things outside of "us." I feel like I am out to sea in a heavy storm, mourning three losses, on a boat, with no radio, no anchor, no island of peace in sight. Alone. Some more.

I am angry. I am sad. I don't want to be either. I want peace.

The path to this moment began with a craving for love, a craving so deep, so strong that I thought if I didn't find it, I might disappear. In fact, I almost did. This is not your typical looking for love story, but it is a story about love. About craving love in a way that transforms you. Craving a love so big it's all encompassing. A love so great it creates more love. It is a story about a quest for love and finding truth. The first truth was in realizing that I was starving.

Love Starved

To Starve:
1. Suffer severely or die from hunger.
2. To want or need something very much.

"I am literally starving for love," she said. My friend, a neighbor, was also going through a divorce. Our daughters were friends. We've known each other for a while, but now we are becoming closer because of circumstance. I knew exactly what she meant by that. I felt the same way. Love starved. Needing something so much that you start to die on the inside from the lack of it. The reason lovers, people, break up, relationships end, and husbands and wives get divorced is because there is a lack of love, an absence of the essential ingredient that makes up a relationship. That is the bottom line. You are starved for love. When you starve, you begin to search for food, sometimes you become irrational, irritable, hungry, weak, eventually you begin to disappear and finally you die.

Have you ever felt that way? Slowly getting weaker, smaller, quieter? That your light was going out? That everything was kind of nothing like, empty of meaning, empty of feeling, just a series of going through motions without the emotion of joy or enthusiasm or love? You wake up in the morning and get up and do your life tasks and you try and bring something to the world but what you really want to do is to get back in your pajamas in your bed and close your eyes? You feel empty and very hungry. Nothing feels completely real. Joyful. Happy. It just is. Not quite horrible but not content either.

"I should have a necklace with an 'F' on it," I said to my closest friend and business partner. "I feel like a fake." She was listening to me go on about the lack of love in my marriage, what he did to make me feel that way, how I didn't like the me that I was in my marriage. How I didn't feel real. How I didn't feel anything. She let me do that a good bit, sitting on her office floor in her basement organizing an event we were putting on. We were together almost daily. After eight years of this, she knew me inside out. She knew the intimate details of my life. Sometimes she'd ask why I put up with it. Why I didn't stand up for myself. Why I didn't say anything and just kept doing it. "What do you want," she would ask. I didn't have an answer. It wasn't so much what I wanted but more, how I wanted to feel. It was hard to describe. And when I tried, it seemed to come out in a language that no one understood. Most of my life looked good, looked right, but there was a big piece of the puzzle missing.

Fortunately, or unfortunately, you can only wear the necklace with the F for a while before the universe issues the "wake up call." This is a message from God, or The Universe, that shakes things up and forces change. My wake up call came in a set of "three" as things often do: a tragic death, near death and the end of a lucrative business. This began the part of the show when my act started to crumble. You know, the "act" we put on for the rest of the world that everything is "perfect" on the outside, but inside our hearts there is a rotten mess. It's an exhausting act.

My husband and I had a nice house, lived in a wonderful neighborhood. I had my own business that contributed to the family income. I was involved in my children's schools, sports, dance and girl scouts. We socialized, we had lots of friends, and we spent time with family. Our life was a perfectly constructed façade with an empty room, the room where love should have lived. Our marriage. Behind closed doors it was a different scene.

Perhaps this sounds familiar. Two people who have ceased to connect. Two people who avoid one another's company. A man and a woman, who 16 years prior professed enduring love in front of family and friends and then didn't honor the contract. Two people who lived in the same house and parented the same children but could not, would not, communicate love. And in the interest of the children, the family, the outward image, they just kept going through the motions on the outside hoping that somehow, someday it would feel better on the inside. The truth is, you can starve a marriage to death. That's what we did. Little by little, we cut off the source of nourishment a relationship needs -- until it was dead.

It took five years to make the moves to end the marriage. It was a long slow death. First, I got sick. Really sick. Hospitalized sick. Almost-died sick. This is what I would call an intense wake up call. Ten days in the hospital to reflect on your life and the things that are important. A month of recovery at home, to be quiet and still. God, or The Universe, or whatever you want to call the higher power that we pray to, look to for guidance (or beg for relief from), signals a need for a change of heart. Forces you to look at your life in a new way. A change of focus.

Unfortunately, that wasn't the only loud wake up call. We then suffered a devastating loss. My 17-year-old son's best friend, his "brother," his first soul-mate, died in a car accident. He was 18, and they'd been friends for 15 years. He was as close to one of my own children as one could be. We were traumatized. All of us. Then my business came to an end, and my partner went back to teaching full time. I lost my sounding board and perhaps my "soft enabler." All this within the course of a year. I felt like the universe was telling me something. Telling me to take a hard look at my life. Wake up. Stop faking it. Stop running through the motions. You are numbing out. Feel something. It's getting shittier, do *something* to make your life feel the way you want to feel. I started by ending the marriage. It had to end. It's sad to admit. It's painful. It feels like an Epic Failure. But it was the brutal truth. We were no longer growing. We weren't even growing apart. We had starved the marriage to death.

Divorce is a death. The death of a relationship and the time leading up to it is like having a terminal illness only without a steady partner to lean on for support. Your go-to person is no longer your go-to. There is no comfort, there is no solace. The person whom you chose to be your soft place to land at the end of the day, who would have pulled you in and wrapped you up and said, "Come here, it's going to be ok," is gone. We'd been gone a long time, though. That source of comfort had died off long before the actual separation. I was dying right along with my marriage. My heart was barely beating. I was starving. We both were.

We suffered severely. I hadn't felt loved in a very long time. I know he didn't either. People get divorced, break up, and separate, but not because of some perceived "problem" with the other person. The bottom line is there isn't any love being given in the relationship. We are born to love and be loved. We were made to couple up. When love is absent, our souls will crave it. I had a craving for love only a divorce would cure.

Deciding to divorce is actually the easiest of the divorce moments. The process of divorce is like being in Hell. Divorce is Hellish. Even the most peaceful divorce feels hellish and mine was extremely peaceful compared to the others I witnessed at the time. Divorce doesn't happen overnight. It can take at least a year and in most cases longer to actually be divorced. And during divorce, there is none of the kind of love you truly desire to be found. The next Mr. or Mrs. Right doesn't show up the second you decide you don't want to be married to Mr. or Mrs. Not Right Anymore. First, you have to admit that you no longer want to remain in the relationship. Then, you have to make all the decisions with the person you are so angry with and resentful towards that you almost rather just off them because it just seems easier than going through this type of hell. You know this is a terrible thought but it creeps in anyway, you just can't help it. You don't just stand up and walk away from 20 years of a life together. There are ties. Big ties like children and houses, families and money. People don't just separate. Things have to separate too and you have to do the work to separate them. Actions must be taken. You have to take them. You have to communicate, which may have been one of the "issues" in the death of your marriage to begin with. Otherwise, the hell just gets worse. It's challenging on all levels. Divorce literally brought me to my knees and some days in a messy heap on the bathroom floor of my newly rented townhouse.

Divorce hurts. Telling the children hurts. Telling your family hurts. Telling your friends, and your neighbors hurts. I craved relief from the pain. I craved love like never before. I had no idea where I was going to find it now. I was in no shape to actually give it. I was empty and exposed. Emotionally dangerous. Was I even capable of love? Was I even loveable? Why didn't I have what I wanted? What had I done to deserve this version of hell? All I'd wanted was to feel good. Solid good. Real.

When the marriage ended, I truly looked like I was starving. There is a picture of me on the Fourth of July where I appear almost skeletal. I hate that picture. It is a picture of someone I didn't know. Someone I didn't like. Not me. At all. Not the Real Me. I was love hungry. Ravenous. I knew I didn't want to stay that way. I needed to figure a way out of this particular hell and lack of love. I wanted to love my life. It took, that dreaded word, time, but I found the way. I want to share it with you, in hopes I can save you some time, some portion of the pain and give you an easier, smoother, faster path to peace and love. And to let you know that you are going to be ok. Happy. Solid good. Promise. During Hell, there are these little tiny rays of light. Set your sights on those miniscule beacons, those glimmers. Therein lies your hope and the truth. Freedom, peace and love, coming up!

This book is a guide to the light at the end of the tunnel. A hand to hold on Friday night when it seems like everyone else has "a somebody" or has a whole normal family. When you are in the middle of trying to find yourself. Think of me as your life preserver, when the waves seem too big to ride, flashing the light and even there pull you along when you get stuck. The conversations here are real. These are conversations I had with men and women going through divorce, break-ups, and separations and starting new relationships. For the purpose of the story, I have put them all together into a he and a she. I share this with you so that you know that you are not alone, so that you may find the peaceful, whole, healing side of divorce or break up, help relieve you of your guilt or feeling of failure for the end of your relationship, or maybe it will spark you to repair the relationship that you are already in – and you can skip the Hell part where "everything sucks" and walk the path to healing, heaven and love. I'm here to open up your heart to love and awaken your spirit. It's a journey to becoming real, to finding yourself, your spirit and truest love. It wasn't always pretty and it didn't always feel good. Truth be told, after the first step, after the "I don't want to be with you another day" conversation, Everything Sucked for a little while.

Everything Sucks

I'm dropping my kids off on the first day of school, and I am scurrying down the walking path to my car as fast as I can lest someone see my face. If I make it to my car, I am safe. No one will know. No one will see that the "always together, always cheerful, always helping out, strong girl, cool mom" is the opposite. She's sad, confused, scared, feeling neither pretty nor strong and absolutely *not cool*. It is a herculean effort not to come completely apart at the seams...and I hear, "Shelly, hey wait." My stomach drops. I hold my breath. My real face would look like the scream mask. But I turn, stop and smile at my oldest daughter's best friend's mom, who (to me) has it more together than all the rest of us, combined. I look at her and I can see, she can tell by the look on my face that I am not ok. I could barely speak.

"Hey," I say.

She asks me if I am ok. The truth just gushes out while tears stream down my face. I feel ashamed, embarrassed, less than. The truth was this, "We secretly sold our house, we are moving into a townhouse, we are separating, our kids don't know." In other words, basically, I am a fraud and failure at being a wife. I am awesome at everything else, but obviously I suck at love. I feel like I am standing there completely naked in Hell. Totally exposed. It's just the beginning of the exposure. My parents, our college age son and the girls in what I call the "circle of strength" are aware of the truth of what's happening. Beyond that, it hasn't gotten out in our supportive and loving village, the neighborhood or the community at large. When you first start telling people you are getting divorced, it is almost an out of body experience.

After exposing myself to her and realizing that I've said the worst and I am still alive and breathing, I feel a tiny bit less hellish. Exposed, but not judged. It was the right person to start practicing telling our story to. She made me feel loved, not pitied, not damaged, not ugly. Unfortunately the feeling doesn't last very long. Pretty much the feeling you have when you first separate is "Everything Sucks," because it does.

"The Talk" Sucks. At some point during the lack of love marathon something will force you to say the words, "We have to talk," and "I don't want to do this anymore." No matter why, how, when, what or who, it sucks. No one wants to hear it and no one wants to say it. It's only the beginning of the Everything Sucks 5K. Before "the talk" there is always some emotional knife thrown at one of the people that sparks the request to talk. During that moment of talking you also question yourself as to whether you really should have said the words. I don't know what's harder, a clear-cut reason for divorcing, like infidelity or abuse, or an emotional distance as wide as the sea.

Whatever the reason, they all just suck.

Living together, knowing you are divorcing sucks. The very being of that person is disturbing. Their existence is unnerving. My soon-to-be-ex moved in with us so that we could get through the holidays without telling our children that our marriage was over. Our plan was to tell them after their February birthdays. It was five months. It was the strangest arrangement but in the interest of the children, we did it. More fake. More farce. More façade. In the name of love for our children. I am not sure it was the right thing to do. But we did it and we all survived. Some people stay in the same house until they can make it work financially. Living with someone you don't want to live with is a supreme test of compassion.

The other "talk" sucks. Telling your children you are getting separated or divorced may be the hardest words to utter ever. They have no idea what is coming. One minute they are playing American Girl dolls and their biggest problem is they can't find the matching shoes to the outfit, and the next minute they are sitting on the couch hearing the words, "Your dad and I…." or "Your mom and I love you very much but…" You might as well be speaking nonsense. Then everyone is supposed to act totally normal like "it's all going to be ok," and no one just threw a bomb into their existence. It is going to be ok, but it certainly sounds like nonsense. Kids are resilient. Things are ok and they adapt to the new normality but for a while, it sucks for them too.

Counseling sucks. But I highly recommend it. We chose to go to counseling to find some peace during the separation, so that our children didn't suffer as much. We were not the only upcoming divorces in our sphere but we were one of the first. We witnessed some really terrible separations that had to have left scars. We didn't want to hurt each other any more than we already had, and we definitely didn't want to hurt our children any more than necessary, so we did something we never did in our marriage. We tried. We tried to work together to establish a peaceful foundation for divorce. We went to counseling. I am not sure that we both had the same goals when we first went. I'll admit I had no intention of reconciliation. My heart was closed to him. We had created a loveless situation and I saw no hope for a future where we were together. Resentment was heavy. But we tried. Counseling is truly helpful, and we were successful at creating the environment we wanted for our children, but sitting in that office holding your marriage, your part in its destruction up to the light does not feel good while it's happening. You feel like a failure, an ugly failure. And you just want it to be different. Different with someone else.

Moving sucks. You can't move quietly without the neighbors knowing and asking you questions. Having to explain yourself is excruciating. I didn't even want to tell the neighbors. I loved my neighbors. We'd raised our kids together, trick or treated together, jumped on the trampoline, had beers on Friday afternoons on the patio, traded popsicles and cups of milk. Our dogs played together. I wanted to disappear in the night and just start over fresh. The problem was I was only going to the next neighborhood over. So I wasn't technically disappearing. I was still going to see my neighbors at school, at the pool, in the grocery. We weren't going into the witness protection program, although the idea of it was very appealing at the time.

On moving day, the truck pulled up and started the two-day process of dismantling my life, sorting my things and his things. I thought

I would be feeling happy, free and liberated. I did not. I hated the movers, I hated my soon-to-be-ex husband, I hated my neighbors that day, I hated everyone that had anything to say to me whatsoever for not being able to make me feel better. I hated them for looking at me in all my exposed failure. Boxes were being packed and labeled as to their final destination – not just which room in the house, but ultimately, which house. It was a huge and overwhelming task. So overwhelmed and angry was I, I left the house that day, went to the townhouse, and basically made my soon-to-be-ex-husband handle the move and the movers. It's his profession anyway. They could handle it. I could not. I was not a nice person that day. I couldn't face the neighbors. I was pissed off. Even though it was my choice. I wasn't enjoying the moment at all. It didn't feel like the kind of freedom I thought I would feel. I walked away like I never lived there.

Holidays and parties suck. As much as you want things to be the same for your kids, family and friends, and even for yourself, they are most definitely not the same. Most likely, you are still wearing your "F" for fake necklace while trying to be socially civilized so that your family, friends and children feel comfortable in your presence. Everyone is uncomfortable though, including you. You wish these precious moments away because they don't feel good. It's virtually impossible to see the joy in any celebration. You smile and have a drink and act like "It's ok, I'm fine." Maybe you have too many drinks, and you say something awful to someone you love or someone says something that makes you feel less than and so you get angry and lash out and you go home and cry, silently begging for it to be different, wondering why. Why me? Why us? Why couldn't we be like them? The happily married couple that talks things out, that shares a partnership, that work like a team, that treat each other with love, respect, care. That hug and laugh and kiss and enjoy each other's company. That smile and dance and have fun together. That accept each other and love each other unconditionally. That make marriage and relationship and life seem pretty easy? What is it about me? What is it about him? What the hell just happened? This isn't the life I wanted at all.

Divorce truth: when you separate, you are basically walking around naked, and other people talk about it. And they give you attention that you don't necessarily want. Looks of pity and "I'm so sorry." There are whispers of *did you hear about*. Sometimes they choose sides and love one person from the marriage and ignore the other completely. There air feels heavy with judgment. Some people drop you altogether just in case it's catching. It's a tricky walk. Sometimes a very lonely walk. You might feel like you've been punched in the stomach and can't breathe. It doesn't last. Promise.

Mediation sucks. However you take the marriage apart, there is work to do. This sucks. You are dealing with precious goods here and as peaceful as we tried to be, there were still times where you wanted to stab the other person in the neck for making you go through this version of hell, for not being what you thought they were going to be, for not seeing you for who you were and appreciating it. This is where the blame part kicks in, and you start hating on a whole new level. Some people can control their hatred and anger and release it in a way that isn't damaging. I watched three very ugly divorces while we were getting divorced. It was painful to watch. I had to keep reminding myself that I chose this. And to reach the end goal, I had to go through these parts. We procrastinated the final ending. I feel like that is unfair to both parties. If you have made the choice to end the marriage, you should follow through in a timely manner so as to set yourself and your ex free. You can't love another until you are truly free and if you even try, it's not wholehearted. Keep the process moving forward. I promise you'll appreciate the feeling later.

Friday and Saturday nights suck. These are date nights. These are the nights when you either have your children or you don't. If you have them you are now a single parent and everyone you come in contact with is a whole family. The absence of a spouse feels like a gaping wound that people can't help but stare at. If you don't have your children that weekend, maybe you are out with your girlfriend and it seems like everyone on the earth is on a date or out with their mate. Spotlight on the divorced person, you might as well have three heads. Or you are home alone thinking. This is not what I wanted at all. I didn't get divorced to be alone. I got divorced to be together in love.

These are the reasons I was in a messy heap on my bathroom floor. My bathroom being the only place I seemed to find any shred of peace. Where no one could see me. The bathroom was my "heaven". My tiny escape hatch from the dark. From Hell. Maybe yours is your bed. Or your closet or your car. The place where you feel the slightest bit safe to show your true feelings. My bathroom was a safe place. In there, no one judged, no one asked questions. In there, I could be me.

"How am I supposed to do this by myself?"
"How did this happen?"
"Who is going to save me?"
"What am I going to do?"
"I'm scared"
"This is too hard."
"I am more alone than I was before."
" I don't want to be alone."
"Everything sucks."

"How are you?" he asked, in that singsong way he does and gave me a big hug.

"I want to kill myself." I whispered in his ear while hugging him back. I know that it's a terrible thing to say. We were at our traditional family New Year's Eve party. He's someone I love very much as a friend. He knows me very well, he and his wife were my business partners. We spent a lot of time together, and I feel safe telling him the truth about how I feel.

He hugged me and said, "No you don't, don't do that. Let's get a drink instead."

"I don't really want to kill myself." I tell him, "What I want to do is kill 'this self.'"

I didn't like the "me" I was prior to my separation, and while I very much wanted to change, I really didn't like the "me" I was at the beginning of it either. I was not feeling good. Barely anything felt good. I thought it was going to feel good. Some part of me thought this: I'll get separated, I'll meet the man of my dreams, we will fall in love, and everything will feel the way I always dreamed it would feel. The truth is, getting divorced is about being alone first. When my attorney said, "Be an angel for a year," she meant, "Be alone." I didn't want to be alone. I wanted to be in love with someone. I wanted to love somebody. I'd already felt alone in my marriage. I'd been alone a long time. This kind of "alone" to me was Hell.

"If you are going through hell, keep going." I opened my mailbox one afternoon and saw the familiar handwriting of one of my favorite girlfriends. She gets me. I get her. We get *it*. The card said, "If you are going through hell, keep going." It was like a smack on the forehead. I like it when God does that; a little smack on the forehead to pull you back to yourself. Inside, I heard a voice say, "Right."

Keep going. I can do that, lying on the bathroom floor in a messy heap is not going to get me what I wanted from this divorce or this life. I wanted to feel good. Solid good. You can't get where you want to go standing still so *keep going*. Note to the people reading this that aren't going through hell, when your friends are, send them cards. Send them glimmers. Send them hope. Send them love. They need it.

While in Hell, I came across a book or perhaps the book came across me. When I get confused or lost, I typically go to books. Usually, the right book falls in my hands at just the right time, with the message I need to hear. When the pain of my marriage became more than I could bear, you would have found me sitting on the floor at the Barnes & Noble in the relationship and self-help section, trying to find answers to all my questions. I wondered why I felt the way I felt, was I the only one feeling the way I felt, and was it my fault. What was I doing wrong? How could I fix it? What was wrong with me, with him, with us, and could it be fixed by reading one of these books? I was sitting on the floor at the Barnes & Noble one morning while my kids were at school. It was the beginning of my separation. I was trying to be a normal person. I wanted to be a happy person. I wasn't feeling happy or normal. A book called *Spirit Junkie*, by Gabrielle Bernstein, caught my eye that day. On the cover was this fabulous looking woman with beautiful hair and a sparkly dress with a big yellow smiley face on it. I reached for it because I wanted to feel like she looked. Happy. Sparkly. Beautiful. Serene. Better than normal.

I devoured the book as only a starving person could do. I highlighted and dog-eared and underlined passages. The book spoke of spiritual guidance, finding your inner guide, listening to your intuition, creating a life of abundance, peace and happiness all based on the basic premise of *love*. The book spoke of prayer and meditation and miracles. Back at home, while reading that book, I got on my knees and started talking it out with God. I wanted peace. I wanted a peaceful divorce. I wanted a loving relationship. I wanted things to be different. I wanted peace and love. *Stat.*

"Be the change you want to see in the world," said Gandhi. It is just as relevant in a divorce, a marriage, any relationship really as well as in life. The truth is, if you want someone to change, the person you have to change is you. If you want a situation to change, the thing that has to change is YOU. It has to begin with you.

While reading *Spirit Junkie* I was turned on to *A Course in Miracles*. It begins with this:

This is a course in miracles. It is a required course. Only the time you take it is voluntary. Free will does not mean that you can establish the curriculum. It means only that you can elect what you want to take at a given time. The course does not aim at teaching the meaning of love, for that is beyond what can be taught. It does aim,

however, at removing the blocks to the awareness of love's presence, which is your natural inheritance. The opposite of love is fear, but what is all-encompassing can have no opposite. This course can therefore be summed up very simply in this way:
Nothing real can be threatened.
Nothing unreal exists.
Herein lies the peace of God.

The Course is a deep dive into spirituality, inner peace and love. The Course says, "First you forgive, then you pray, then you are healed." I didn't understand forgiveness so much, and I kind of prayed, but most of all I wanted to be healed. Healing meant Heaven. Heaven = Love. I wanted that. It also stated very clearly, "Only love is Real." I took The Course very seriously.

Forgiveness

"Forgiveness is the key to happiness"—
A Course In Miracles

Dropping the F bomb. "Walkie-talkie anyone?" I post on Facebook. This means, who wants to go for a walk around the neighborhood and talk things out? It's an hour walk. It's like therapy, but free. I get a lot of responses when I put up that post. Some are excuses why someone can't walkie-talkie, but they want to, could we do it sometime soon. I get takers too though. So we lace up and hit the neighborhood loop and start to chat it out.

"He's driving me crazy," she says. Then tells me a story about a recent interaction with her soon-to-be-ex. It brought up a lot of emotion, frustration, pain. I listen. I get it. Sometimes, I am the one that uses up the whole hour. Today, the hour is hers.

"I am still so angry with him."

"He's never going to change."

"This is all his fault."

"You're right," I say. We need validation for our feelings. And her feelings are her feelings. Who am I to say they are wrong?

"What am I going to do?" She asks.

I look her straight in the eye and say, "Drop the F bomb."

Tell him to 'F' off?" she asks, and laughs.

"No," I say, "Forgive him."

"I can't do THAT," she practically screams. "He doesn't deserve THAT!"

"I know what you mean." I smiled. "We could egg the house instead."

This makes her laugh, harder. I am serious about the F bomb though, not the eggs.

The whole *forgiveness* thing can be baffling. It is a hard concept to grasp. You hear about it a lot. There are books and quotes and chapters in the Bible on it. You might have heard it is the only way to peace, the only way to be happy. You might not believe it, but there is a whole lot of truth in it.

Unfortunately in most situations, we are *so* wronged, *so* offended, *so* right about how we feel that we just cannot do it. Just *cannot,* until the other person sees what they've done, suffers at least mildly, understands and either publicly or privately admits to inflicting the pain. They must accept the blame for all that is wrong in our world. Right? Your ego is very much against the F bomb. Your ego very much wants to use the other F bomb and tell him/her to just F off.

"What if that is the one thing that is holding you back?" I ask her. "What if in this moment you just said, 'OK fine, I forgive him,' and everything was instantly different and you felt solid good. Misery ended."

She gave me a serious look. "I can't."

"Ok, what if he never admits his part? Do you stay miserable forever, in hell forever because you are right?" I ask her a serious and very important question from *A Course In Miracles*, "Do you want to be happy or do you want to be right?"

Popular thought is that by offering forgiveness, we let the person or situation that wronged us so wrongly "off the hook," when we fully believe they shouldn't be off the hook or deserve our forgiveness at all. Ever. Someone must be punished for the pain they inflicted and it is our job to punish them. But really, is it *your* job?

Through The Course, I dug deep into this whole concept of forgiveness, resentment, pain and the path to peace and happiness. I needed to understand it. Forgiveness means "to give forth everything, to not hold on to anything." That includes giving up fear, guilt, pain. Forgiveness is largely misunderstood. It is meant to bless. It is a call to sanity by offering love instead of guilt and pain. Forgiveness though is not a bargaining tool. Saying "I forgive you," while also meaning *if you will give me something in return*, or, *to relieve my own guilt,* is not true forgiveness.

Forgiveness should lead away from anger, condemnation and comparison. Forgiveness means what you thought the other person did to you did not occur. It doesn't pardon mistakes or actions and make them real. It lets the mistake, action, or injustice, whatever you want to call it go. Forgiveness opens up your mind. It is a release. Forgiveness is quiet. It does not judge. It accepts the truth exactly as it is without judging it. Forgiveness is letting go of the past and remembering only the love you gave and the love that was given you and then forgets all the rest.

Epic fail. "It is 100% my fault that the marriage failed," he said. He was another friend still working through his hellish part. It's important to talk this stuff out with others who have been there before you. It helps bring light to your dark.

"You can own your part," I said "but it's a 50/50 split, so you didn't fail. You got a C."

"I got a D+ at best." he says, shaking his head.

When a marriage ends, it feels like an Epic Failure. The truth is it is never one person's fault. Both parties contribute to its destruction.

Both parties participate in the lack of love party. It's a circle of blame. I did this because you did that and I did that when you did this and I felt like this because of that, so I did that – until finally you can't take it anymore and you say the words that you think will release you from the hell. "I want a divorce." In other words, "I'll take the F."

The part forgiveness plays here determines whether or not you get an A in your next relationship, the Retake. If you haven't made peace with the divorce, the marriage, yourself and the ex-partner, you might as well go back and repeat the assignment. You can't carry guilt, resentment and pain into a new relationship. If its love you want, you have to be in a loving mindset. You have to come pure, without the baggage of the past; otherwise you are absolutely going to experience a reenactment of the demise of your first marriage. You have a year to work on it, don't waste it floundering around and wallowing in self- blame and self-pity.

Own your part. Forgive it. Fix yourself and move on. Try and show up a better version of yourself next time around.

Peace. "Resentment is like drinking poison and hoping it will kill the other person." I was poisoned. I hoped my ex would die from it or at least go away because of it. He didn't. He just stayed there, fueling my resentment. You have a choice in every situation, a position of strength. You can stop giving that person, those thoughts, that situation or the past your precious energy. The peace is there right after the forgiving. I am not saying you have to tell the person they are forgiven, but you can. That's *super* powerful but not necessary for it to work in your own life.

What is very effective, though, is forgiving it in your own mind, in your own heart. Tell yourself that you will no longer let this person's actions, your thoughts or that situation have the power to hurt, anger or pain you. You just won't. Every time you forgive someone, a relationship is healed. It takes practice, but is worth the effort. *Remind* yourself of it often. Put it on a sticky note on your dash, your bathroom mirror, and your wallpaper on your phone, your screensaver.

I forgive _____.

Say the prayer, "Forgive him, her, them, *me*, they know not what they do, they've done, I do, I've done."

Let God, or The Universe, take care of it for you.

Free yourself.

Forgiveness doesn't ask for proof that the person is now innocent. Let them be innocent. Let yourself be innocent.

I programmed this reminder to pop up on my phone and my calendar every day at noon, so I wouldn't forget. "FORGIVENESS IS THE KEY TO HAPPINESS." Two years later, it still pops up at noon. Even my kids know it.

As forgiveness becomes your habit, you become more peaceful, more open to receive love and happiness. Forgiveness is a true release of the past so that you can enjoy and embrace the present and experience a joyful, happy future.

Forgive the past. Forgive the choices that didn't serve you, that no longer serve you. Forgive past hurts. Forgive yourself. Forgive the Ex. No matter what the circumstances are. It's a gift to you, a gift of peace and a lightness of being. Forgiveness equals relief. Release. Freedom. Peace.

I used a visualization I learned in *Spirit Junkie* to go with releasing a relationship. I figured I could use it in my forgiveness practice. I was willing to try anything to find my peace, so while sitting on my bathroom floor, I visualized releasing him. I visualized a big black cord connecting us. I visualized taking a pair of scissors, cutting the cord that tied us, and watching him float away. After a while, I could very much see it, and then I could very much feel it. I felt much lighter. The lighter I became, the more miraculous things became. I forgave everything and everyone. I forgave a whole lot, not just my soon-to-be-ex. And then I learned how to pray.

Pray

It's Friday evening; our kids are with their dads. My also-separated girlfriend and I are sitting in my kitchen. I open a bottle of wine, pour two glasses, turn on Pandora, do a little "Friday Happy Dance" and sit down across from my friend.

"Yay!" she smiles a little and holds up her glass.

"Yay!" I smile my "I'm trying" smile and hold up my glass.

We sip and sing along to the songs.

"I love this song." I sing out loud.

And she laughs because I say it 1000 times a day, and she says, "You love all the songs."

"They're what get me through, they are like my prayers," I sing as I turn up the music a little louder.

Fridays feel weightier than the regular days. Weekends can feel lonely to the extreme. We've become each other's "weekend companions." Our friends are all out as couples tonight. We do not get invited to "couple night." We don't even want to go out tonight. Staying home and drinking wine together feels safe and pathetic at the same time. Wine and girl talk. Good stuff.

We talk it out a lot. Our separations, impending divorces, our soon-to-be-ex spouses, children, dates, men, love, hopes, wonderings. As much as we enjoy each other's company, we still want that someone to love and love us, the way we want to be loved.

We clink our glasses. "I just want it to be different," she says, and her eyes tear up a little. This makes mine tear up too. Not only am I a sympathy crier, I feel the same way she does, and sometimes it feels like time is dragging. I turn down the music. We sit quiet for a bit, sipping our wine and then I ask her if she prays.

"How the hell is that going to help?" She laughs, that kind of laugh you laugh when you're sad or mad or not quite feeling it, and you want an answer that is a lot more tangible like, "Let's try getting on match.com." A problem solving answer. Quick magic kind of answer. Not a, "Maybe you should pray," kind of answer.

"I promise you it will change how you feel about things," I tell her. "I want it to be different too. I feel like its coming. My different. I feel different and I think it's because of the sense of peace I feel when I pray. I've asked for help from something bigger than me, because I believe there is something more powerful than myself that I can access. Believe me when I say, I didn't even really know how to pray, but I think its working."

I believe in the Divine. God, the Holy Spirit, Jesus, angels, heaven and hell. Buddha's ideas, A universal power. A oneness that exists among us all. A power greater than myself. I am not religious. I don't have a specific religious teaching that I follow. I've always believed in God as the higher power, but I wasn't a "worshipper," so to speak. I don't go to church on a regular basis. I don't read the Bible. I read biblical verses on Pinterest and in blogs or books, but I have not studied the Bible. Honestly, I have always been a little bewildered by the church-going people, the Bible-quoting people. My ideas and beliefs don't always line up there.

I struggle with an image of God as a giver of guilt, as a punisher, as a judge. I know people with strong religious beliefs and traditions, and I respect them. I respect their commitment to their religious faith. I just don't understand the people who think they know God better than anyone else. Or feel that their version of God is the *right* version. I understand the "holier than thou" people even less. The people who judge your faithfulness by church attendance confuse me. I don't understand the people that talk the talk but don't walk the walk, therefore I struggle with parts of the church experience. I fully support the idea of church as a place for spiritual education and learning the foundation for strong spiritual faith. I love the music in church. It's a revelation. I enjoy some religious rituals. I have come to learn how to pray the rosary. I appreciate the lessons of it, the truth, the fruits of the mystery. I find it healing and comforting. I believe in faith and love.

I have resisted "religion." But I have faith, and I pray. Before this divorce and all the challenges leading up to it, I prayed in my own made-up sort of wishy-washy way. Not really on my knees, but in my head. Kind of. Sort of. I said thank you at the end of the day before closing my eyes. I asked God for things like protection over my children, healing for sick friends, but I never really went very deep, deep enough to ask for guidance and peace and all things God promises us. Nor did I pay a lot of attention to what God might desire of me. Surface prayer I would call it. As I started my ascent out of hell, I needed a deeper prayer. I found this meditation in *Spirit Junkie*. To me it sounded like prayer, and I figured it was a good enough place to start. I felt like I could trust her, this woman, this author, coach, person I would like to be like, with the big smile, promoting happiness and spirituality in a way that I could grasp. She had a real relationship with Spirit/God/The Universe. I wanted it. I wanted real. So I sat in my bathroom (my safe place) in the morning before everyone got up, criss-cross applesauce, hands on my knees, eyes closed and started my days like this:

I feel new.
(breathe in)
This day is going to be unique.
(breathe out)

I feel at peace.
(breathe in)
This day is going to settle some stressful issues.
(breathe out)

I feel in harmony.
(breathe in)
This day is going to be free of conflict.
(breathe out)

I feel creative.
(breathe in)
This day is going to show me something I have never seen.
(breathe out)
I feel loving.
(breathe in)

This day is going to soothe differences and include those who feel left out.
(breathe out)

I feel whole.
(breathe in)
This day is going to flow seamlessly.
(breathe out)

I added this to Gabrielle's meditation:

I am defenseless.
(breathe in)
This day I do not have to defend myself.
(breathe out)

I added this because I figured if I became "defenseless" then the tension in my house, in counseling, and in mediation would be less palpable. If I trained myself not to respond with defense, there could be no defensiveness. Peace was bound to come. I started using that meditation not just to start my day, but also before mediation, before I walked into counseling, before social events, before sitting down to dinner, before conversations with my soon-to-be-ex. Anytime we had to interact. I'd close my eyes and focus on my breathing and take the 5 or so minutes it took to bring myself to a peaceful demeanor. After a while, I started using it whenever I was in an anxious state. It became my anti-anxiety "drug." As I became more peaceful, peace rippled out. I didn't just meditate though, I also got on my knees closed my eyes and said a prayer to someone I didn't really have a solid relationship with yet, and started each day with this:

Thank you for this day you have given me.
Thank you for all of your many blessings.
Forgive him for he knows not what he does.
Forgive me for I know not what I do either.
Please guide me.

Yes, right there on my bathroom floor. I started a prayer practice that I ultimately built into a daily ritual and turned into a constant conversation, because after I started praying. I started to change. The more I prayed the better I felt. The more I prayed, the better everything felt. And the more I prayed, the more those around me changed, too.

The God Box.

I'd heard the phrase "Give it up to God." I did not really understand it, but then someone told me about putting your worries, your pains, and your wonders in a little box as a way of letting them go, as a way of giving them up to God. I liked that idea. It was tangible. Especially when I was obsessing on something. I have this pretty little box now that my friend Lavonne gave me with cookies in it at Christmas. I've given these adorable little prayer boxes out to other friends. When I find myself latching on to a situation or I am giving too much of my thoughts, my energy to someone or something, I write it down on a slip of paper and put it in the box. I write the person's name or the problem I think I have on one side and "God" on the other. A postcard to God to take care of things for me so I can move on without the mind lock.

It's interesting to check the mail in the God box after some time has passed and reflect on God's answers. Like the Beatles sang, "There will be an answer. Let it be." Put it in the God Box and Let it Be. Check back later, and you will see evidence of how it all played out in your favor. It may not have felt good at the time, but you either learned a life lesson, or you witnessed Grace.

It's a practice.
Becoming prayerful was not completely new, but I did take to a whole new level. I began a constant conversation with God, or the Holy Spirit, depending on the situation or the moment. I pointed to the sky a lot and said things like "Thanks," and smiled or gave the peace sign, which meant I appreciated an answer, a moment, a song on the radio, a good feeling, the rush of energy or the peace in my heart. It meant I was noticing God's presence. God likes to be appreciated. Just like we do.

I also sometimes looked to the sky and just questioned. "Really God? What the F?" Or I said things like, "enough already," when things got really heavy. The more I practiced prayer, the more I began to see more of the love in every situation and less lack of it. Or I guess I should say I looked for the love not the lack of it. Where there may have been a perception of lack of love, I came to understand that that was where I was supposed to be more loving.

I depended on God a whole lot more. I depended on God, all the time. The Course told me this, "There is nothing to fear." And "God's voice speaks to me all through the day." I believed it and I wanted to hear it. So I prayed and I listened hard. One of the ways I feel like God speaks to me is through books. I found these prayers in a book called *Outrageous Openness*. Best. Prayers. Ever. If you ask me.

"If you wish this (thing, situation, job, relationship, action), I cannot do this on my own. But the perfect route is already selected so if this is your will, fling open the doors, if this is meant to be please bring the right help." Afterwards, you must be patient and wait for the answer to come. Have faith, it always comes.

"My perfect path is already selected and will arrive at the right time. I will be shown the steps to receive it." That doesn't mean sit on the couch and wait for stuff to happen. It means take a step and watch how gracefully things begin to fall into place. There will be people who offer you the answer, the next right move, the opportunity. A hand reaches out to help you. You have to keep walking forward though.

"Follow the steps as they appear, you'll be shown the way."

"Let what wants to come, come. Let what wants to go, go. If it is mine it will stay. If not whatever is better will replace it." This is the hardest one to adhere to, especially when you want something, or someone, so very much. Here is where you have to dive deeper and pray a little more, to be able to let that thing/person/job/situation/relationship go so as to receive the highest outcome. Even if it feels uncomfortable. Trust that God is your source and you are always safe.

"If there is a road I should walk, help me find it. And if I need to be still, give me peace for the moment. Whatever your will can you help me find it?"

These are prayers I say in all situations, when there are decisions or when I am feeling unsettled or disconnected. The Course gave me many prayers that could easily bring me back to a sense of peace and safety. While doing the 365 lessons in the workbook, I set my phone to remind me hourly each lesson. These lessons stuck with me, as they were meant to. I have found that the one I need either comes to mind easily or if I reach for The Course, I automatically turn to the page that I need to hear the most that day or in that moment, phrases like:

"Above all else I want to see."
"Make me ready."
"God's answer is some form of peace."
"In fearlessness and love I spend today."
"Happiness is my only function." (That's my favorite.)

The secret of true prayer, though, is that you forget the things you think you need and ask only, "Thy will be done." As The Course says on prayer, "The real sound is always a song of thanksgiving and of Love. It is a stepping aside, a letting go, a quiet time of listening and loving. And it is to Love you go in prayer. Prayer is an offering; a giving up of yourself to be at one with Love. There is nothing to ask for, because there is nothing left to want."

Prayer felt good and so did "Rehab."

You Heal

"If there is a loss of cabin pressure, the panels above your seat will open, and oxygen masks will drop down. If this happens, place the mask over your nose and mouth, and adjust it as necessary. Be sure to adjust your own mask before helping others."   In other words, take care of yourself first, before you take care of everyone else.

Rehab and creating your own "bubble"
There should be a Betty Ford Center for divorce. Since there is not, I've created a program for healing. If all divorced people went to divorce

"rehab" before entering a new relationship, the second marriage divorce rate wouldn't be 75%. You must take care of *you* first during a divorce. It's imperative. It sounds selfish. It's hard for the "givers" of this world to embrace. It's this or check yourself into The Betty and that will probably run you about $40,000 or more. I hope that by reading this book, I can save you at least $39,985. You must heal the wounds and deal with your own insides in order to be whole again before starting a new Love relationship. It will also make you a better mother, father, friend, sister, brother daughter, son, overall, a better human.

I am familiar with alcohol and drug rehab. I have alcoholics and addicts in my family. They've been to those wonderful places of serenity. When I dropped my 19 year old son off at Father Martin's Ashley for 30 days, following his downward spiral into prescription drug addiction, after the tragic deaths of two of his best friends within two years, I hugged him tight and said, "I want to stay here too." The thought of having someone else take care of things while I talk it out with people, get lots of therapy, get creative with art, sleep, get quiet, pray and stare at the water sounded heavenly to me. My son calls rehab "the bubble." I call it a reconnection with Heaven. It's a great place to be. It's healthy. It's safe. It's all about you. Extreme self care.

The bubble looks like this: Healthy meals prepared three times a day. No alcohol, no drugs, no caffeine. no sugar. There is nothing that would create a chemical imbalance to affect your self-awareness. There are routine bedtimes and waking times, lights out at 11 pm and everybody is up at 7am for breakfast. No skipping breakfast. You must attend daily individual therapy sessions and group therapy sessions. No electronic devices. No cell phones. No internet access. No television. Nothing to interfere with or distract you from your well-being. You aren't even allowed to spend time with the opposite sex. No triggers. You may read books, but only books that are about personal and spiritual growth. There is spiritual leadership. Prayer. Music. Art. Creativity. Meditation. Exercise. Yoga. Positivity. Accountability. Sharing. Human Connection. Listening. Support. You are surrounded by a tribe of people who have the same goal, to get well. My son says everyone should go to rehab because it's really about creating a better you, and less about being "an addict."

Since there isn't a rehab for divorce, you have to create your own bubble. It's the only way to truly recover. When you get out of drug and alcohol rehab, you are told to "work your program" to maintain your sobriety. It is the only way to stay sober. In order to maintain your sanity and continue with the healing process while going through a divorce, it's best to "work your program" daily, too. Separated and recently divorced individuals are emotionally dangerous. My therapist calls it "legally insane." It would be easy to fall into the same relationship patterns or fall for the first "superman" or "superwoman" that takes you to dinner and a movie, if you aren't careful and aware. Take the time to heal. I promise it will be worth it.

I fell into a recovery plan for myself that included all this: therapy, personal growth coaching, journaling, prayer, meditation, reading, soul searching, self help books, loads of girlfriend time, yoga, Pilates, healthy eating, sleep, massage, and human connection. The year of your separation should be devoted to getting you well, before devoting yourself to another love relationship. My end goal for this was to heal up and prepare my heart to love wholly. It might take longer than a year, but if you follow the program, a year is all you need to strengthen up that precious heart. I call this the year of extreme self-care. You deserve it, especially during the "everything sucks" part. Treat yourself the way you want to be treated. Love yourself the way you want to be loved. You deserve to come apart and come back together stronger, wiser, and more loving than ever. The only way to come back stronger is to take extra good care of *you*.

Extreme self-care basics, a.k.a. checking yourself into "The Betty."

1. Developing a Spiritual Practice

"Can you imagine what it means to have no cares, no worries, no anxieties, but merely to be perfectly calm and quiet all the time?" asks The Course.

To me, that sounded like a dream and I am all about dreaminess. Spirituality promises just this. Peace. The only way to true peace is by opening up your mind to a spiritual practice.

Connecting with the Universal Guidance/God/Higher Power/Spirit whatever you want to call it opens up a whole realm of peace and strength for you to draw upon, not only in a time of need or healing, but in your everyday life.

Prayer is communication with God. Prayer is opening your mind, in quiet, so that you can hear God's voice. Prayer is giving thanks to God for his gifts. Gifts like peace, friendship, hope, joy, love. Prayer is where you ask your questions. I have found that starting my day with God goes a long way to my peaceful demeanor. I show up for God. God shows up for me. I begin the first hour of the day with a prayer, the same one I've always gone to: *"Thank you for this day you have given me, and your many blessings."*

Then I lift up names of people I know and love that are in need of God's grace. God knows their needs, so I don't have to ask for specifics, just for God to know that I have joined their prayers. After which, I record my "gratitudes" from the day before in my journal, and then I read and reflect on what God wants me to hear that day. I find these answers in *A Course in*

Miracles. The first year I was studying, I followed the workbook. Now, I turn to pages at random and take that lesson for the day.

Part of the morning ritual is meditation. My meditation is simple. I recognize the Holy Spirit abiding in me. I am quiet. I focus on my breathing. I focus on a lightness of being. It is an opening of my mind. I do this before I start on my journal.

At the end of the day, I say the same prayer. I ask for forgiveness for my mistakes and the moments my peace was disturbed. I ask for strength and for any words I need to sleep on. Honestly, I look forward to my morning ritual so much that sometimes I just want to go back to bed, so I can get back to the learning part.

2. Therapy

The Course says, "The purpose of psychotherapy is to remove the blocks to truth." Basically, it is a relationship created to remove your walls, your barriers to the truth in you. The goal is to heal your mind. Illness is sorrow and your guilt. Healing is actually a form of forgiveness. A therapist can help you to identify all that hasn't been forgiven in yourself. That hour on the couch gives you an opportunity to look at yourself, your part in relationships, your walls, your blocks, open them up to re-evaluate. The end goal being self-forgiveness, release from the past, and healing your mind. A strong and healthy mind is just as important as a strong and healthy heart.

3. Coaching and personal growth

"I wish I had met you 10 years before I got divorced," said one of my clients. "You could have saved my first marriage." I sought all kinds of guidance during my separation. Therapy, spiritual, friends, books, blogs and a professional life coach. I used that year of "being an angel," as my attorney referred to it, to learn about myself and take a good look at my heart, my blocks, what I wanted from my life. I dug deep, with my coach, to clarify how I wanted to work, what kind of work I wanted to do. I questioned why I felt stuck, why I wasn't feeling fulfilled. I wanted to find my sweet spot. What I loved doing, and what I wanted to do with my time. My personal growth coach helped me realize my sweet spot was connecting with people and empowering them with the tools to create better relationships. People began to come to me for inspiration, for lessons in love, to find peace.

I imagine you are feeling stuck, unloved, less than peaceful, a bit on the failure side too. Coaching, personal growth workshops, and seminars all contribute to opening your mind to finding the best in you. Helping people find their spark, is what sparked me up. Standing up and speaking about finding your spark, speaking about love, lit me on fire. There is something that will light *you* up, too. Coaching can help you find it. Coaching is not just for finding your best work, it is for all areas of your life. It brings all your areas into balance, while you work on the ones that are keeping you off balance. It also helps you maintain balance in your life.

4. Exercise

I highly suggest a fitness routine that creates a strong mind-body connection. Pilates and Yoga create an atmosphere of peace and focus. Of the principles of Pilates, concentration, centering, control, breathing and integration contribute to centering the mind. Focus on breathing, and the creation of a calm body and spirit. It is the method of exercise that I chose, mostly because of the peaceful atmosphere found in the studio. Gyms overwhelm me. Pilates requires guidance. I needed a guide more than a run on a treadmill. Yoga promotes mental clarity, helping you think more clearly, and opens your heart space. As Yogi Charlene Wederbrand, said during our session, "A closed heart is not open to possibilities and our potential." During times of high stress, exercise, especially these, provide a much needed endorphin rush. Pilates and yoga healed my soul, strengthened my core and settled my mind. I also find that running/walking outdoors is as much a meditation as seated quiet meditation. Running with my favorite songs infuses my spirit with bright energy. Music pumps me up, lifts me up, and keeps me going – not just during exercise. If you're going to get addicted to something that makes you feel good, go for the exercise. The other alternatives are counterintuitive.

5. Healthy Eating
You are what you eat. If you are eating crap, then you are going to feel like crap. Simple.

Strong minds are well nourished. Healthy minds are well nourished. That goes for hearts too. Eat well. Make this a priority, but not an obsession. What exactly does healthy eating look like? As close to real as possible is a good measure. A long list of "added" ingredients is an automatic no. Lots of water. Fresh fruits, vegetables, and protein. Caffeine, sweets, treats and alcohol in moderation. The magic cure at our house is always water. "Feel cranky, feel tired, feel yucky? Drink some water," I say. Try not to skip meals. Hunger anger a.k.a. being "hangry" is a chemical imbalance. You can control your balance. Food is part of staying balanced. Which brings me to the next very important item during "rehab."

6. Keep Your Chemicals Balanced
Unnatural chemicals, substances, or patterns that unbalance your natural chemicals create a "negative" reaction or response when interacting with other humans.

Sugar. Avoid sugar as much as possible. Sugar crash is a real thing. I don't mean never have dessert. Personally, dessert is one of my favorite pleasures. Eating a whole sleeve of thin mints won't make you feel good. Your rational brain knows this to be true. Eat to feel good about yourself.

Caffeine. Being over caffeinated causes anxiety, insomnia and irritability. Insomnia causes anxiety and irritability. Anxiety and irritability cause us to react and respond negatively in situations where we might otherwise have been peaceful.

Alcohol. We are all pretty well schooled on the effects of alcohol. Alcohol intensifies emotions, decreases control and the ability to make logical decisions. A drink or two won't get you into trouble. A lot of drinks will. And a lot of drinks often will lead to bigger problems. It will also keep you from processing your feelings.

Drugs, prescription and otherwise. I'm not saying don't take your prescribed medicines. Seek professional help if you feel you are unable to balance out with natural methods. Sometimes we need prescription drugs to get us back on keel.

Using drugs, food, or alcohol to numb our feelings has an adverse affect. You can't numb out one select feeling. You numb your ability to feel any feelings. Therefore numbing out pain, also robs you of joy. Numbing out sad, numbs out happy. Try instead to process the negative feelings so that your heart is open to feel the positive ones. Keeping your chemicals balanced creates the environment for a peaceful mind and a happy heart. You can't function at your maximum potential when your chemicals are unbalanced.

7. Beauty Sleep
"Sleep is the best meditation"- Dalai Lama XIV
Sleep deprivation is a form of torture. We are not firing on all pins when we've deprived ourselves of restorative sleep. Your whole body including your skin goes into repair when you sleep. Lack of sleep contributes to heart disease, heart attack, diabetes and depression. Don't torture yourself. Go to bed.

8. Quiet.
Treasure your alone time. Create times of peace and quiet. Stillness. Ultimately peace is found within ourselves. If you don't covet your alone time, see number two and get to the bottom of why you don't want to be with yourself. The only way to really know yourself, know your

own heart is to spend time with yourself in quiet. This is where it is easiest to hear God. When you care for someone, you enjoy their company. You want to spend time alone with them. Love yourself that way, spend time alone to acknowledge your pain, release it and love and appreciate your own beauty. Rest, heal and recover.

"One has to be alone, under the sky, Before everything falls into place and one finds his or her own place in the midst of it all." -Thomas Merton

9. Massage

I started getting monthly massages during my separation. Before that, I only went when my body was in crisis. A locked up neck, an excruciating pain in my upper back, or an intense headache. I would arrive in tears, suffering, practically begging for healing. I would be healed for the moment, and I was told I needed to come back for more regular massages to really benefit, but I didn't until I was in crisis again. I found a lady at the Asian market near my catering company that I swear was magic. Between the separation and the new business, my stress level was on overload. Thirty minutes with my dear Mena was a piece of Heaven. I hugged her every time. Then I met Chris at the Pilates studio. I found a level of healing massage I hadn't ever experienced. When I returned from Florida after my mom died, I went straight from the airport to the massage table. I increased the massages to twice a month and added them when I wanted to get a sense of grounding and peace. Massage is a form of release. I know now when I have emotional pain, release is necessary. Chris, at Studio Be Pilates, is a master. I count on him as much as I do the therapist.

It is estimated that ninety percent of disease is stress related. Nothing increases the aging process faster than high stress. Massage alone won't alleviate stress entirely, but adding regular massage to your routine of self care does lead to:

Decreased anxiety.
Enhanced sleep quality.
Greater energy.
Improved concentration.

Increased circulation.

Reduced fatigue.

Massage clients often feel a renewed sense of perspective and clarity afterwards. I couldn't agree more.

10. Grateful+Attitude= Gratitude

Start each day with a grateful attitude. You create your reality and your vibe. Give a good one – for yourself and then for the others around you. There is always something for which to be grateful. Choose gratitude over complaining. You will begin to feel the difference.

11. Journal

Keeping a daily record of your "gratitudes," as I like to call them, serves as both reminder that there is always something to be thankful for and a moment of praise to God for the gifts of the day. Be they "little" or "big," God appreciates our appreciation. I began the gratitude journal when I first entered "Hell." A blog post I'd read on *Owning Pink* suggested it. Each day I wrote down 5 things that I was grateful for.

Understanding that I was always grateful for my children, my health, my home, my work, and my family. Looking back, there were days I wrote I was grateful for my yoga pants and that my favorite white t shirt was clean. In this way, I believe I was grateful for some level of comfort. As I progressed through the year, my "Gratitudes" began to lean towards the people who showed up that day. I started really noticing all the people and how they were so generous, loving and kind. Recording our thoughts and feelings can also help us end unhealthy behavior patterns or correct our mistakes. It helps us to see where we get stuck, where we hold back, where we might show up better next time. It also helps us process the emotions that we are carrying.

It is best to feel your feelings and work through them. Doing so privately can be a strong part of the healing process. In this way you are not venting your feelings on another and creating a situation of attack, blame or guilt. Journaling gives you the space to release any and all of your feelings in a safe non-judgmental space, perhaps another way of "giving it up to God." I re-read my journal on New Year's Eve the first year. I was alone. My kids were with their dad. I was home in my room (my sanctuary). I was struck by how much love and kindness was offered by so many people. I felt very loved and very blessed and not one bit lonely.

12. Get Creative

While my son was in rehab, art therapy was one of the experiences he felt the most positive connection to. Creating something with your hands gives your mind a rest. A change of focus. A breath of fresh air. Getting creative doesn't necessarily mean you have to create art. Here are some ways to "get creative" at home:

Cook or bake. Immerse yourself in the choosing of recipes, shopping, chopping, measuring, cooking.

Reorganize a closet, drawer, room, garage.

Repaint a room, recover a piece of furniture, make something old into something new.

Sew. A quilt, a shirt, an outfit, a pillow.

Plant a garden. Dig in the dirt.

Make a piece of jewelry or many pieces.

Grab some markers and doodle, color in a coloring book.

Write a story. Write a song. Write a poem.

Make a collage or vision board.

Get your hands busy and free your mind. Buddha says, "Chop wood, carry water."

13. Human connection

At rehab, you dine with people three times a day. You have group therapy. You have individual therapy. There are lectures and discussions. There is church. Our souls were created to connect with other souls. Spending time alone is good for the soul, but too much time alone can be debilitating. Seek company of people who fill you up. Who spark your heart. Who love you and you love. Spend time with your tribe. Go help out somewhere. Anywhere. Lend a hand. Just be with people. Being with people is healing. Giving of your heart is healing.

14. Get to know yourself.

This is the most important part of healing. Chances are, you've been everybody else's something for a long time. Mother, wife, sister, daughter, friend, employee, boss. Those roles define us, obligate us. Spend time digging around inside your own heart and figure our what lights you up. What floats your boat and what doesn't. Sort out the things you do for others that give them joy, and understand if your joy is there too. Let go of things, obligations, activities that no longer serve you. Strike out on your own. Eat the food you like, watch the movies you want to watch, do the work you want to do, do what you want to do. My friend always laughs when she is with me and someone asks me what I do. My answer is always this, "I do what I want." Most of the time my time is spent doing what I want. Sure there are tasks, and papers and stuff that is requested of me that I must complete, but for the most part, I do the things that I want to do. My work is something I want to do. That makes me feel good. Most of the time, doing what I want lines up with people, so we do what we want together. This includes my kids, friends, family, neighbors, clients. Dig in. Find out what sparks your heart, and do it. Allow yourself to be yourself. Allow yourself to please yourself.

When you leave rehab, they tell you that the secret to your success as a human free of addiction is that you have to "work your program." Consider this your 14-step life-loving program. It isn't just for divorce, it's a human program, a program for living a peaceful, joyful life, a life you will love.

The End Goal: Be Well. Be a Good Human.

One Word: Tattoo It On Your Life

"Pick a word." I said, "one word to describe how you want to feel at the end of this challenge." I was leading the personal growth part of a 30-day wellness challenge that included Pilates, health and nutrition coaching, and personal growth at the Pilates studio. I was speaking to the group about the power behind achieving their 30-Day wellness goal. About focus, and about attracting that "one thing" into their program, and ultimately into their lives.

"Make that word the first thing you see everyday and the last thing you think about at night. Put it on your phone wallpaper, sticky note it on your computer, at your desk, on your dash," I suggested. "Live it. Embody it."

On a larger level, I do that. I choose a word to live out for a year. The word each year comes to me just about the time a year is ending. It's personal, not random. The first year, I had just finished the "separation year," and I'd sold the catering business I had with my sister, so that I could pursue a career in coaching, speaking and writing. I made a commitment to using the word in all situations, all relationships, all parts of my life. At the end of the year I tattooed it on my wrist. *Love.*

By choosing that one word, I set an intention of being more loving and finding the love relationship I craved. I felt like it needed laser focus. I'd dabbled in dating a little, but wasn't feeling that amazing, bright, blow-your-mind kind of feeling. The one that makes your heart feel like its on fire. The one that makes your eyes sparkle when you speak of that person. The one that makes you light up. Not only that, I wanted more than a love relationship, I wanted to love my life, not just love the way most people think of it. More than romantic love, for and with just one person. I wanted the experience of having more love in my life as a whole, of "loving" life and being more loving to all the people in it.

There were "hard" things going on. My son's next closest friend died in a terrible car accident and he was spiraling out of control with grief; my mom was diagnosed lung cancer, the third time she'd had cancer; and we'd lost a lot of money in our catering business venture, not too mention I was still getting divorced. I wasn't sure how we were going to weather it all. I knew there was something more powerful in myself that I hadn't tapped into. I wanted more joy, to be more loving to the people in my life, to connect on a deeper level, to love what I was doing with my life. To love my family, friends and people more deeply. Not only was I craving love, I was craving depth.

Love is a big word. It's scary. I am not going to lie, I got scared sometimes. It was frightening for some people, this year of "love." They didn't get where I was coming from. It was suggested I "tone it down" so as not to scare away any potential suitors. It was mocked. It's ok, I joked about it too sometimes. My use of the word made some men very uncomfortable, as if it held too much expectation. I held my ground. I kept *loving* it all. I tried to come from a loving place, no matter what the situation was. No matter how I was perceived or how others perceived me. I tried to find the love in every experience, every day, good and bad. It took practice. Sometimes I forgot. I told people I loved them and I meant it. I loved things for other people. I forgave old wounds. I forgave new situations that hurt. I looked for love in those situations too. It was an incredible learning experience to say the least.

I took it to the biggest level and the tiniest. Even in my Pilates practice. I refused to say, "I hate ab work" (honestly I do). Instead, I would say "I love ab work." If I found myself starting to use the word hate, I would replace it with love. I put the word all over my house. I have love t-shirts, love bracelets, books with love quotes. Some might think I OD'd on Love. I had to. It was part of the experiment. Part of the plan.

"All doubt and despair and fear become insignificant once the intention of life becomes love." – Rumi

Heaven

"There is only one path to Heaven. On Earth, we call it love." – Karen Goldman

"Stop sending me the crybaby emojis," I text late one night. "I hate the way I feel," she texts back. "Then don't feel that way."

"I'm lonely."

"You're not alone. Your kids are there."

Then I get the emojis that have the tongue sticking out or the eyeballs popping out.

You can only feel one feeling at a time. You get to choose which one you feel. Why choose one that didn't make you feel good? You are in charge of your thoughts, and what you think becomes your reality. Every day, every moment we have a choice about how we feel. How we relate to the world. What kind of face, attitude, demeanor we share with the rest of the world. No one is responsible for "making you happy," or "making you feel less lonely." That is your responsibility and yours alone. You always have a choice.

In an instant, you can change the thoughts that keep you in Hell to ones that take you straight to Heaven. An instant. The Course asks, "How long is an instant? As long as it takes to re-establish perfect sanity, perfect peace and perfect love for everyone, for God and for yourself."

This is called the Holy Instant. If you are still living in Hell, you are doing at least one of these things:

Living either in the past or in the future instead of being present now.

Feeling guilty about your past.

Worrying about your future.

Not letting go of the past, or repeating the past by bringing the past to the present and projecting it into the future. A.k.a., staying stuck in your story.

Disliking some aspect of your life, of yourself, but not doing anything about it, and then blaming everyone else for how they are making you feel.

Denying yourself love in the present. Neither giving love, nor being open to receive it.

Making your circumstance your identity. Bottom line, your self worth is tied to your past, an event, or an idea that doesn't serve you.

"Hell is what your Ego makes of the present. The belief in hell is what prevents you from understanding the present because you are afraid of it."
- A Course in Miracles

How to get to Heaven when you're feeling like Hell
Be present. Be here now, doing what you are doing right now, with whomever you are doing it with, not silently planning the future or fretting over the past. Pay attention. Fully. With

all of your senses. Enjoy now. Deal with now. Handle now. Live now. Be grateful for now. Say, "Right here, right now," when you feel yourself slipping away.

Live in the moment. This moment is brand new. Fresh. Full of possibility, hope. No past, no future. Just now. Yours to "enjoy the sh*t" out of or feel the pain of. The last moment is gone. Let it go. If it sucked, move on and be open to the next best moment. If it was awesome, celebrate it. Note it. File it in the "moments to remember" file in your heart. My beautiful friend Lilienne once told me a story about seeing her son try on his wedding attire. She said, "I took a picture with my heart." Even better.

Go with the flow. Be more like water, less like rock. Stop trying to control situations, control the future, control what people think of you, control everything. The only thing you have control over is how you repsond to anyone, anything. The rest is out of your hands.

Let go. Let things come to you. When you feel like hell, you are usually trying to "make" something happen, make someone see, make something be the way you "want" it. What's meant for you will come to you effortlessly, but only if you let go of this control. If you are busy trying to control everything, something beautiful, amazing may pass you right by. Remember, "Thy will be done." Whenever I get spun out, it's always a matter of me forcing my will on something. In this moment, you might hear me say, "Surrender, Dorothy!"

Forgive. We did a whole chapter on this. If you didn't get it then, go back and read it again and get it now. In every instant where you feel like attacking someone, release them. When you forgive every situation, every person that you feel is against you and forgive the past, you release yourself from hell. Instantly. Stop feeling guilty and forgive yourself too. Guilt is Hell. Give that up once and for all. If you feel like you have wronged someone. Apologize and move on.

Be fearless. Of the past and of the future. Neither really exists. The past is gone and the future isn't here yet. Why are you fretting over it? Commiserating with it? Be fearless of the present moment. It's going to pass. In joy, in pain, in pleasure, in guilt, in love, however you choose to experience it. How do you want to live this precious moment?

Love you. Love yourself first. (If you don't, then get back to 'The Betty.' Believe that you are most lovable, because you are.) Then shine that love out to everyone. Give it fearlessly, generously. Accept the love of others, however they give it, and appreciate it when they give it to you. The more love you give out, the more you will receive – and there is no place for hell in love. Only perfect peace and happiness. This goes for all relationships, not just one special one.

"It's Hell," he says, "This time between 40 and 50." He's said this before. He's at the beginning of a divorce. I see where he is. He's mad at his life at the moment. He seeks me out. I am a glimmer of hope for him. We are standing in my kitchen, which seems to be where all the issues of the heart come to be discussed. Where love and truth is served. "That's not true," I say, "I can't believe in 10 years of self inflicted hell. I am in my 40's, 48 actually, and I am the happiest I have ever been."

"Why?" he questions, eyebrows up and with a tone that implies impossibility. "I've been working on it, I figured some things out. This is a good time in my life, one of the best." I smile. He wasn't having it. Trials for sure, divorce, death, illness, and pain. We all have "stuff." But I am mostly happy, peaceful. It's been a time of great personal growth and deeper human connection. There are beautiful amazing moments to be experienced in all of this growth. Massive evidence of great love, feelings of deep peace, overwhelming joy, beauty. Miraculous moments.

"The person you have been is not the person you will remain.
Think of that as both a challenge and a gift."- M.H. Clark

The Transformation
"You're so different," she said, and her eyes grew large. "Tell me one word you would use to describe yourself now."

"Transformed." I said instantly.

"I can see that. That's the perfect word."

We were "hiding" out having dinner. She likes to "hide" out in obscure places, so that when we talk we aren't interrupted by people we know. It had been months since we'd gotten to talk like this. There was a time when we both read *More* magazine. We went straight to the "Reinvention" article. It gave me a great sense of hope that I could change, that things could change and we could still be whatever it is we wanted to be, that it was never too late.

"Tell me how you feel."

"I feel different. I feel peaceful. Happy. Like everything is OK. Like my enthusiasm is back, my yellow balloon inflated. I feel like a great weight has been lifted. I feel real. Like now we can wear the "R" for real necklaces."

She laughed but she knew it was true.

Being real is so much easier than maintaining an act. A show. A façade. Being real is what being in Heaven is all about. Free to be. Free to be you.

Faith

"Do you believe in all that?" He pointed to the cross at my neck. I deflected my truth by saying, "My kids gave me the necklace for my birthday, my daughter thinks God is a she."

I'd never worn a cross before. Like I said, prior to the divorce and creating my own rehab,

I had a tenuous relationship with God and religion. I was surprised when they chose the cross. I realized as I answered that I hadn't fully committed to faith. It was a moment that changed me. I know that some people are uncomfortable with religion, and that it might have changed how he was feeling about me in the moment, that I might be judged. I didn't like how I answered then, but I have deep appreciation for the question now, because it caused me to explore my spirituality and to embark on a path to getting to know God, and an overall experience of deepening faith. One way God speaks to us is through other people. God was questioning me. I appreciate the moment, and him for asking.

"The certain are perfectly calm because they are not in doubt. This holds them in perfect serenity because this is what they share." – A Course In Miracles

Miracle Mojo

"The Universe always has my back," I say. And, "God always takes care of me." I like to point these moments out to people when serendipitous things happen or when it looks like my life is "charmed." I like to tell the story about when I lost my cellphone at the hockey game. It's easy to grasp. I have a lot of these kinds of stories but this one is the least "out there."

My girlfriend and I are at the hockey game. We go to the ladies room during one of the period breaks. I always carry my cell in my back pocket of my jeans. I always put it on the toilet paper holder so it won't fall in the toilet. We left the ladies' room and ran into my daughters' jump rope coach and her husband. We got to talking, we ordered a drink, we talked some more. After about 30 minutes, we went back to our seats.

As we stepped into our row, I put my hand on my back pocket as is my habit, and I realized my cellphone is missing. I turned and looked at the stranger in front of me, and said, "Oh man, I lost my cell phone."

She says "REALLY!" Like that. A Big "REALLY?" And I said yes. She holds out my phone and says, "I found a cell in the bathroom. Is this your cellphone?" I scream "YES!" Because it is, and because I think it is so damn awesome that The Universe just brought me my cellphone. I say, "Thanks! The Universe always has my back."

She looks at me with big eyes and asks, "What did you say?"

And I say it again. "The Universe always has my back."

She can't get over that whole statement. For the rest of the game, every few minutes she leans forward in the row and looks at me and gives me that "that was so cool" face. As we leave the match, I stop and hug her and say thank you for finding my phone. She asks me my name. I say, "Shelly. What's yours?" She says, "Charlotte," and I laugh because of course it is….that's my daughter's name.

There's more where that comes from, maybe another book on "The Universe has your back" concept alone. No matter what is going on at any given moment, I have full faith that God's got us. I have learned that God only wants what's best for us, and what's best for us is love and peace. To that end, we will be directed to whatever it is that will serve us to a greater good. A happy outcome to all things. Peace is the purpose. The means to peace may not always line up with what we think the means should be, but we will get there, guaranteed. Everything, every experience is pushing us towards a greater good and a deeper faith. In that way, you can go along peacefully and joyfully loving people and your life in the moment or you can be like Eeyore in Winnie the Pooh.

God does not punish, God does not strike, God does not will us to be hurt, suffer, sacrifice or feel pain or loss. Therefore we have been given miracles to save us. What is a miracle? The Course says this:

An expression of love.
Everything that comes from love is a miracle.
Miracles are healing. They supply lack.
Miracles bring more love to both the giver and the receiver.
Miracles are thoughts.
All miracles mean life.

Miracles undo the past in the present and thus release the future.

Miracles demonstrate it is as blessed to give as it is to receive.

A miracle is a service: "Loving your neighbor as thyself."

Miracles reawaken the spirit.

Miracles represent freedom from fear.

A miracle is a universal blessing from God through you.

Miracles honor your loveability. They only see the light in you, and release your mind from your mad illusions about yourself.

Miracles strengthen your spirit.

To bring on your Miracle Mojo:

Pray. Through prayer, love is received, and through miracles, love is expressed.

Be in Love. Have a loving mindset.

Make miracles a habit.

Devote each day to miracles.

Forgive. Accept God's forgiveness as you extend it to others.

Be grateful. Miracles should inspire gratitude.

Love everyone the way you love yourself.

Love yourself the way you love everyone.

Miracles come from a miraculous mindset.

The Ripple Effect

You have the power to uplift the world around you. Sending loving thoughts, blessings, and your good vibes out to the people in your life has a positive effect on them. You can do this through meditation or prayer. We have the ability to affect our atmosphere with our own vibrations. Radiate positive. Radiate love. Radiate joy.

I see it in my children, my friends, and my family. As I became more peaceful and loving, they became more peaceful and loving. We are all connected by spirit. You can even change your relationship with someone just by sending out good vibes, using that simple prayer/statement, "Forgive him/her for he knows not what he/she does." It will change your mind about how you feel about someone. My friend and I have come to say, "Oh, I think they need a hug," when we witness someone being unkind or losing their peace over something. In that way we mentally send them a little love and a blessing of peace. We laugh about it, but we laugh with love. We've come to understand that there is little to complain about, to be upset over in this life and lots to love and enjoy. Hug it out, we say.

Loved

"Your task is not to seek for Love, but merely to seek to find all your barriers within yourself that you have built against it." – Rumi

Perfect Love

"There is no perfect love," she said. I am on the safe sofa. The therapist's office. She's been sitting across from me during the entire journey, from moments before separation to present. We are having the conversation about where that last bit of my heart is not open.

My immediate thought is, "God's love is perfect."

With that thought, I realize how deep my relationship with God and Spirit has become because that is exactly what perfect love is. God's love. A love that bears no judgment, always forgiving, sees no sin, sees us only perfectly, loves us only perfectly, and because of it we are loveable, beautiful, ever loved and ever safe. We were created in the image of God, therefore we should love only perfectly as well.

Perfect love is unconditional love. There was a time when I thought only children were the recipients worthy of unconditional love. The truth is, everyone is entitled to your unconditional love. Love is not, "I will love you if you love me this way." Or, "If you do this for me, serve this need, I will give you my love." Unconditional love means you have my love, under every condition. It means there is nothing you can do to make me not love you. Like God's love, all is forgiven. That doesn't give humans license to misbehave. It means I will love you forever, no matter how messy you get. I will love you through your mess. I don't have to participate in the messes you choose if I choose not to, but I will love you. There is total freedom in unconditional love.

You don't have to be prettier or thinner or fatter or softer or smarter, or richer or anything-er. You get to be you. Loveable you.

"I wish you loved you the way I love you." I say to my friend. "I wish you saw you the way I see you."

"You are beautiful, loving, soft, smart, caring, fun to be with, silly, thoughtful, kind. Why don't you see that? Why do you base your lovability on the acceptance of one person instead of the love of all the people around you? If you weren't so much goodness, do you think I'd choose to spend so much time with you?" She was hurting over how she felt she was being treated in a relationship. She wasn't feeling loved by that person, and therefore unloveable, and she was losing faith in ever having what her heart desires. I was getting wound up.

I get wound up when I am very serious about someone and their lack of vision about themselves. Tears streamed down her face. Because I love her, it hurt me. Because I know that she is all those things and more, and I know that somewhere along the way someone stole her "perfect." It happens to all of us. Somewhere along the way, someone, your mom, your dad, your high school boyfriend, a friend, a non-friend, a coach, someone important in your being, steals your "perfect" and then we spend a great deal of time searching for the one magical person who will give it back or expecting the person we are in a relationship with to give it back to us. The person who will make us feel we are beautiful, loveable, good enough, smart enough, *perfect* again – and promise to stay there reminding us and meaning it.

Some people decided they don't have to have their perfect back. Instead, they just spend a ridiculous amount of money on vanity, or spend a ridiculous amount of time working to make the kind of money they think will prove they are perfect, or they will just put on a perfect façade to cover the scar, "the soul sucking wound," as I like to call it. That one deep scar that f's up our relationships, that makes us have anger issues, leads to addiction, problems with people, problems at work, problems with our ability to relate and communicate purely, strongly. It is our weakness. Our fear. Our last barrier, our ego block to love.

Perfect love is loving ourselves the way God loves us. You should love the person in the mirror first. This is where God shows up, in the mirror. Unconditional love is given to you by you, from God. Marianne Williamson writes this in her interpretation of The Course, "The only beloved who can always be counted on is God. The ultimate partner is a divine one, an experience of ourselves that is totally supportive and forgiving."

You are perfectly loved. Just the way you are.

"You're so mean when you talk about yourself. You were wrong. Change the voices in your head. Make them like you instead. Pretty, pretty please, don't you ever, ever feel, like you're less than, less than perfect, like you're nothing. You are perfect to me." – P!nk

Friend Love

My phone buzzed. I was in the car on the way to the airport. "I am having a weak moment," she said, and I could hear tears in her voice. She's my closest friend, neighbor, confidant and companion. The gift from our divorces is this friendship we have created. We'd driven to and from Florida for spring break with our daughters, where we discover my mom is much sicker than she let on. I am on my way back to take care of her.

"I just wanted to say thank you and I love you. Thank you for taking me to meet your parents and for being a good friend and for loving me."

"That's not weak," I say, my voice just as heavy with emotion. "That's strong."

It made my heart swell. Expressing our feelings and our love for each other is never weak. It strengthens both parties. It's a communion of love. This is what binds us. The Course says we should, "Make our brotherly love relationships more romantic and our romantic love relationships more brotherly." It is not weak to say, "I love you." Love only strengthens, never weakens. Getting on that airplane I felt stronger because of her love.

After my mom died and I returned home, I spent one evening in my bed crying and asking God why I always had to go through hard things alone. Why was I always alone? Did I really have to do everything alone? Where was the man, my partner, the person I was supposed to be able to lean on? The one God promised to hold my hand. I was very upset. The night before the service honoring my mom's life, my cousin arrived from San Francisco to stay with me. He is my mom's brother's son. We spent three days laughing, driving, singing, and talking. God showed up in my cousin Joey. I was not alone.

When my dad died three months later, I left the hospital alone, wondering again, why alone? I drove home to an empty house, put on my pajamas, poured a glass of wine and sat down on my sofa and sent a text to "the man."

"I am home, I just poured a glass of wine. I don't want to be alone. Can you come?"

My phone buzzed with a text that said, "I'm coming over. You better let me in or I am crashing down your door." That made me laugh, and smile. It was not him, it was my friend

Kathleen, the business partner I'd shared my life with for eight straight years. The one who I hid with to have dinner, the one who pried open my heart all those days we worked together, who I joked about the necklace with the F with. She was perhaps the only person on the earth who might "get me" in that moment. She'd lost her dad, years earlier. We spent a couple of hours talking it out, laughing, crying. God showed up in Kathleen. No one else could have made me feel the way she did that night, nor understood me in the way that she could.

God showed up again the next morning and took me for a walk, a walkie-talkie with my friend whose parents were both in heaven now too, someone who loved me and could relate like no one else. Every time I asked, God sent the person he thought best filled the need. They weren't who I thought they were supposed to be, they weren't in the form of just one person. But they gave me the love, laughter and peace I needed at the time. Whenever I ask, "Who is going to take care of me?" God always does. When a human doesn't show up, that's when I know, at that moment, it's up to me to take care of myself.

Circle of Strength

"I just love, love," she said as we were hugging each other in the parking lot of the funeral home. "It's the only thing getting us through this stuff you, know? Our love," I said into her hair. It was a wake for one of our closest friend's father. A week earlier, we'd been at the funeral for her beloved grandmother. Sitting in these churches with my girlfriends lining the pews, passing tissues, squeezing hands, singing *Ave Maria*, tears rolling down our cheeks for our girlfriends suffering losses, I realize how incredibly blessed we are to have each other. The strength of each other. That no matter what comes our way, we are strong because of each other. When I look around, they are there. To hug it out. To make us laugh or smile through the tears, to hold us up.

That's why we are here. To love each other through. There are fifteen assorted women in our "circle." I am the oldest and the only one who didn't go to the same college with the rest of them. My sister is my link to the group. Having babies at the same time is what gave me the entry into a very tightly knit bunch. We've been a circle for a little more than 20 years.

Some were friends before "the circle," and the relationships that were born in high school and in college have grown deeper ever since. It's a long, beautiful, colorful story that at some point will be shared, but for now its purpose has always been support, love, comfort, strength in numbers with a whole hell of a lot of laughter, joy, silliness, and shenanigans. God promises He will not leave you comfortless. The queens of comfort. A safe circle of love, where you can lean in, lean on or, if you hit the floor, will get down there with you and remind you to breathe.

Tell Them How You Feel

"The beautiful relationship you have with all your brothers is a part of you because it is a part of God himself." – A Course In Miracles.

I shared this story on Facebook after a funeral for a 24-year old young man whose family I've known for most of my life. I find funerals to be a most beautiful, emotional and true moment. I've learned much about love and living your life from the people who have passed away and the people who loved them in the past few years. Someone once remarked that I've been to a lot of funerals lately. I suppose God is using these moments, these people to teach me some important stuff to share. God knows I am listening and also that you are listening to me when I share.

As with all funerals people stood up to speak. That morning, four young men stood in a packed standing room only church and talked about love. They stood up there with cracked voices, tears on their faces, hearts wide open and said, "I loved Andrew and what I loved the most about Andrew was that I knew that he loved me."

Boys. Talking about love. Unafraid to show their hearts, unafraid to stand up and tell the truth. Saying "I love you." and talking about their love. It created more love in that church, more love and more peace. Andrew had become a part of them, and they shared Andrew's love with everyone else. It made those young men stronger, not weaker. I was proud of them.

During the year of love, I set an intention of deeper connection with people. It started with a birthday message. My friend Kathleen always made us go around the table and say something about the person whose birthday it was. At their core, people want to be seen. It feels incredible to hear how people see you and they feel about you, what you do that makes them love you so. I took it a step further, and started writing that out on my friends Facebook walls on their birthdays. I've included some of the birthday "posts" at the end of the book. The purpose was to let people know that they were important to me, that I loved them and appreciated their love for me, that I could see their essence. It felt just as incredible to write them as it did to hear it from my own friends.

Tell people you love them. Tell them what they mean to you. In the book *The Fault in Our Stars* by John Greene, one of the characters invites his best friend and his girlfriend to his "pre-funeral" funeral. He knew he was dying. He'd asked them to write his eulogy. He wanted to hear what they were going to say about him when he was gone. He wanted to know how he was seen.

When my mom was in her last days, we asked people to send us messages. I read every single word to her. These messages were the most loving, tender, heartfelt messages. On her last day, we called people and let them say goodbye. She couldn't speak, but we were told she could still hear and every single person said, "I love you." Loving thoughts surrounded her to the very end. Let the people you know and love know how you feel about them, now. Don't wait until they are gone. Tell them how they inspire you, how their love and friendship make you feel, what they mean to you. Love them now.

Special Love

"You can't make one person solely responsible for delivering your happiness." I said. "You have to find joy in yourself, in all of your relationships, friendships, family relations, not just that one person. It's too much pressure on that person. It's too much weight. It's not fair to her."

We were swinging on swings on the beach, talking about his last girlfriend. He was looking for that next special person. He was looking for love. Weeks later he messaged me and said, "I can't stop thinking about what you said, thank you. I did that. I was doing that. It's so true. I am not going to do that anymore."

Special relationships are ego driven. Without the ego, all would be love. In our past we learn to define our "needs." Then we look for that one "special" someone to fill those needs and to make us feel worthy. When they don't fill them as we see fit we make the "special" person feel guilty for not filling the need. *A Course in Miracles* teaches this, "The ego seeks to use a relationship to fill our needs as we define them. The Holy Spirit asks that the relationship be used by God to serve His purposes, and His purpose is that we might learn how to love more purely."

The Holy Spirit uses these "special" relationships as learning experiences so that you may learn the truth about yourself. That love is in you, that happiness, joy, and peace all abide in you. You do not have to look outside of yourself to have your needs met, to take love guiltily from another. Faith in the love within you means you do not have to seek for it from "someone special." The ego is in relationships only to get something. The ego believes that it can get and keep by making the other person guilty for not giving the other what they need. In the "special relationship," one person thinks they have sacrificed something for the other, and hates him/her for it. He is not in love with the other at all. In fact, he is really in love with sacrifice. The Course teaches that, "Whenever you are angry, you can be sure that you have formed a special relationship that the ego has blessed, for anger is its blessing."

It is important to recognize that "special" relationships can also be formed with friends, parents, children, or others – not just our "significant other." Our children, our friends, our parents, our family members are not responsible for making us happy, or creating our joy. They can bring us joy, share their love, evoke positive feelings in their presence, but giving them power over our happiness or unhappiness or our peace is making them "special." Relationships share feelings. They do not expect.

Holy Love

"The Holy Relationship is chosen by spirit as a plan for our reconnection with Love."
– A Course in Miracles

In the words of Augusten Burroughs, "If you meet somebody and they love you when you are your true, awful, not ready yet, boring, not cool enough, not handsome enough, not pretty enough, too fat or too poor self. And if you love them back so much it makes you calm. And they have flaws and you don't mind a single one of them, that means you get you to the church and you pull one of those priests out of bed and you have him cast one of those wedding spells on you. Because if you found that, you found IT."

The goal of the Holy Relationship is truth. God created his relationship with us to make us happy. Because of this the function of relationships is to "make happy," the holy relationship shares God's purpose. Each person has to look within themselves and see nothing lacking. Two whole happy people come together and shine that love and happiness outward. That doesn't mean you come together needing the other for your happiness, or to make the other person happy. It means you share happiness with each other.

We were made to couple up, to be each other's salvation, to help each other along the path to peace. It is a common state of mind where both are forgiving of each other's errors so that both may be happy. To have each other's back. The holy relationship is strong, and has the power to heal all pain. The function of the holy relationship is a joining of the minds. What one thinks the other experiences with him. from loving minds, brings joy and gladness. The holy relationship is a shining example of the power of love that makes all fear impossible.

"I want what they have," she said. "I know, I do too. They are here to show us what it is supposed to be like. That's why God made them our friends," I said. "I don't want to take from her. I just want someone like him. Gentle. Happy. Kind. Loving," she said. "Someone who takes good care of my heart, like he does for her and she does for him."

We have a couple that we spend a lot of time with. It's their second time around. They love each other for real. They are real. To me it is so obvious why God chose them to be together. In the aftermath of her divorce and the break off of his engagement they are exactly what the other needed for protection, safety, peace and love. They are a shining example. They embody togetherness. They found a safe place in each other, and it shows by the light in their eyes and their kids eyes. They bring joy to each other and those around them because of it. They both came from disastrous relationships. They found what we all are promised. What we all deserve: a safe place to rest your heart. It's divine.

"Now everyone dreams of a love lasting and true. But you and I know what this world can do. So let's make our steps clear that the other may see. And I'll wait for you. If I should fall behind...wait for me"
– Bruce Springsteen

Make Me Ready for "That" Love

"The will to win is not nearly so important as the will to prepare to win." – Vince Lombardi

"You can prepare your heart for love," I said. "I don't know, Shelly. I am not so sure about that." He tilted his head and looked at me in the way that said *tell me more, even though I am full of doubt on that subject.* "Why not? I am doing that. You can do the inner work on yourself, figure out your 'stuff,' so that the next time around you are better. You can show up better. Like getting better at sports."

He's "the man" I've been spending some time with. We are talking about closed up hearts. He's an athlete and a coach. Athletes and coaches understand the process and principles of training, coaching and learning how to work as a team. You can apply those principles to life, to relationships, to work. You can do the work, the training to better yourself but in order to learn how to love in a relationship you have to be in a relationship. Be on the team. *Want* to be on the team.

Relationships are assignments. Relationships are where we have our highest personal growth potential. When the issues arise, when your ego starts to invade or take over, or when your crap, or your "less than," "not good enough" part of yourself starts to surface in a relationship, it is a teachable moment, a lesson for your own personal growth. It's where your blocks to love reside.

Relationships should be like a lab. The best, most successful relationships are the ones where not only is there great pleasure in each others company, but also a lab-like environment where two people help each other reach their highest potential. They have to want to be on the team, though, and do the training, i.e. "work in the lab." That means facing the challenge moments, digging into the assignment and communicating, listening, empathizing, forgiving, showing up and being fully present. That means facing your fears at the kitchen table, and talking it out without your egos, without attack and without blame. You have to be willing to move through the discomfort because the stuff is going to show up, no doubt about that. Your block to your highest state of pure love is going to emerge so that you can grow out of it. You can quit that relationship, that team, but it's just going to show up next time around until you finally deal with it for good. Marianne Williamson said, "It is through another person we can come to know ourselves." Your partner is your mirror, reflecting the beautiful and the ugly. God always pairs you up with the right lab partner.

We have come to a defining moment in our relationship lab. "The man" and I. Things outside of "us" are dramatic, therefore fears have arisen. We have not been giving our best selves. We've been giving parts of ourselves. Sitting across from me is my Really Big Relationship Assignment. I've chosen this moment. I've asked for this conversation. I've asked to sit down and face my fear, the fear that if I tell him how I really feel, he won't accept it. I could have walked away, quietly, without a fuss. Just forget the whole thing and move on, because that would be easier than facing what's really going on. I can't disregard the two hearts, though.

We are always guided by God/The Universe to the relationship with the greatest learning opportunity. "No one is sent by accident to anyone," says *A Course In Miracles*. I've been "preparing my heart" and my mind for moments like this. I've been asking God to "make me ready." Therefore, I know I have been put here on purpose. Across from me is a man whose spirit I love. I see nothing but his goodness. I've walked in the door after saying a prayer for the truth, and the right words to come out of my mouth. I am trying not to get confused by my own ego nor bamboozled by his. Egos are loud. Spirits are quiet. It's not easy to recall all the training, what you've learned and what you even teach, when you are sitting in the hot seat. We were in a teachable moment. We were smack in the middle of the petri dish sitting at the kitchen table in relationship lab. I am being asked to communicate what I want. How I feel. What the purpose of this relationship is? We both are. We are trying, because the truth is we care for each other very much.

The Love Story You've Probably Been Waiting To Hear

"You do not need anyone to light up your life. You can do that for yourself." – unknown

During the year of "Love" I did fall in love. Not once, not twice but three times. First I fell in love with 'the man,' next I fell in love with God, and then I fell in love with me.

The Man and Me

I'd come out to meet one of my girlfriends, also divorced. I walked in the restaurant and he was seated next to her. I sat down, introductions were made. The moment I looked at him, my head said, "Do not audition." And I promptly turned the other way to meet the couple on my left and spent the rest of the evening, spreading my attention a little heavier on the left side. Hours later, the man and I left the building holding hands and ended up talking until dawn. For the next few weeks, he did exactly what I wanted a man to do. He lit me on fire. He was wild and free with his thoughts. He didn't hold anything back. He showed me his soul-sucking wound and I showed him mine. We craved each other. He did a cannonball right in the middle of my life, and proceeded to question everything about me. The things I wasn't true on, not yet sure of. He pushed me emotionally. He scared me to death. It was exhilarating and terrifying all at once. One night, just a couple of weeks after we'd met, my girlfriend stopped by to give me a gift she'd gotten me for my birthday, and found me sitting on the steps in my foyer in tears waiting to hear from him. "What's wrong?" she asked with concern.

"I don't want to feel like this," I said quietly, tears streaming down my face, "it's too scary." "Here," she said, "open this." I opened the gift and it was a bracelet that said, "Embrace the Journey." Divine intervention, I say.

The desire, the emotion, the connection was irresistible. That first night we met, we talked until the sun came up, and he told me things that made me want to know everything about him. He asked me questions that reached deep into my soul, and when he spoke I could hear myself. There was a part of me that I was missing, I saw it in him, and I wanted it. He was the first man to ask me, "What do you want from me?" Since no one had ever asked me that before, I hadn't even thought about it. I answered with a simple, "Just show up." His response was, "That's the one thing I can't do. I am so emotionally unavailable right now."

He shoots straight, that's for sure. I'd like to say I was smart enough, emotionally grown up enough to turn away, because emotional availability was at the root of my craving. I should have run, but remember, there was fire. Instead of turning away, I ran right into the flames. When he sat on my sofa eight weeks into our secret love fest and said, "The therapist says we should wait a year, that one of us will probably hurt the other."

I immediately replied with the solid truth, "I have no intention of hurting you."

"I just want to be with you. What's better than us? Why do we have to wait," he asked, with his arms wide open across the back of my sofa. I still conjure up that moment now and then. He was so open and sure. Confident. Three things I was lacking in that moment. All I could say was, "Right." I was terrified. He was in

Hell. He was newly separated and a love-starved maniac too, like both of our therapists said, we were "legally insane." I was getting close to reaching a point of legal sanity but neither one of us was legally or emotionally free just yet. He hadn't done the "angel year." Neither one of us was legally divorced. But we desired each other in the fiercest way. So we proceeded to do what two insane people do. We messed it up within 24 hours. 100% total sabotage. 50/50 split. And it hurt us both. Hurt like a mother f**ker. And we couldn't bring it back. There were half-hearted attempts but nothing real. If we hadn't messed it up though, the next best thing wouldn't have happened. It got really personal, between God and me, that is.

"Pain and change are the keys that open the door to a deeper understanding of the our human experience." –Debbie Ford

God and Me
The sharp ending of that relationship was the impetus for an even deeper relationship, my

relationship with God. I had nowhere else to go but to my knees. My relationship with "the man" was private. Secret, actually. I was a mess of emotion. I was confused, angry and upset with God. I thought I was getting the partner I was promised. The love I waited for. My perfect fit. I wanted to know why God gave me this man that made me beautiful and fired up my soul – and then snatched him away so abruptly? I wanted answers, stat, and so began my education in real love and the holy relationship, the special relationship, brotherly relationships and the most important relationship of all.

This was the relationship I truly needed, the one with God. The relationship whose foundation would strengthen me in every other relationship I have. Especially for the next relationship assignment, for every trial and for every loss that came after it. The closer I got with God and the Holy Spirit, the easier it became to handle things outside myself. And the things kept coming. Big things. Things like addiction, death, trauma, grief and Really Big Assignment- Round Two.

Just Me

To be totally transparent, even though God and I were hot and heavy for a year, I still wanted "it." Don't we all? Every group I speak to, every person I coach, every woman and man I meet ultimately want "it." Relationship connection. The holy relationship that God promised. The one to "walk together in peace and love with," to take their last breath with. The one I'd been preparing my heart for. My prayer had become, "Make me ready," and so I expected God to drop that man right down in front of me soon.

I'd done my "angel year" and a year of serious studying, learning, growing. I'd learned my lessons (I thought). I'd prepared my heart (I thought). I grew in faith. I trusted God's plan. I tried not to make anyone "special." I felt whole, mostly happy, pretty much complete on my own. Now I wanted the icing on my cupcake. I began asking, "God, am I not ready?"

So the Universe does what it does to "test" all the lessons you have learned. It gives you "The Really Big Assignment" or in my case, "Really Big Assignment, Round Two." My friend and I like to call the lessons that repeat themselves, "Groundhog Days." If you don't learn the lesson the first time, it shows up again until you get it right. It might not be with the same person, but it will show up again and again until you respond fearlessly and differently. Or it might be the same person in their better version.

"The Man" came back, waving a tiki torch and using my own words to pull at my heart. Honestly, I'd been waiting and hoping he would. And *oh my god*, did I want him back. I hadn't stopped wanting him. I'd reached for him a few weeks earlier when my mom was dying. I wanted the comfort of a human bigger than me. Stronger than me. His kind of comfort. He delivered. Still private, but there with me. This felt almost all the way good. Then it happened again, a moment of truth, where we stopped short. Both of us. His heart more open this time but maybe only a crack. Mine more open but still closely guarding that secret garden that Bruce Springsteen sings about. I kept him just short of seeing all of me. He lit me right up again. Another 8 weeks in, we ended up in the lab at the kitchen table in that "what do you really want" moment. I told almost the whole truth. I could verbalize the ending, but not the middle. I tried, but what came out was part my version and part what I thought he wanted to hear. A little ego and a little spirit mixed together. Hours later, we both left the building, we left smiling but not holding hands. Peaceful and happy with our progress, but not together.

"All you want is to dance and sing," he said as I was leaving. "That's the truth, and all I ever want for you is for you to feel good." I sang and I smiled and danced out the door. That night he sent me a text that said, "Are you alone?"

"Are you checking up on me?" I text back. "Yes." In his way, he was making sure I was ok. I said, "I am, but I don't feel lonely. I feel good. I hope you feel good too." I did. I felt *solid good*. I did not want to let him go, and I missed him like crazy for awhile after that delicious moment, but Mr. Really-Big-Assignment-Round-Two taught me some juicy stuff like it was supposed to. I am proud of us, and I love him for it.

My sister said it best when she said, "You are not doing what you teach everyone else to do in your programs." Mr. Really Big Assignment (rounds one and two) made me look really hard at my own heart, and my own actions. My expectations were not of him but of myself in a relationship, and there was personal work left undone. I wanted him to show up for me in a way I wasn't showing up for myself. I was still keeping one part of me hidden and closed. I needed to figure out what I was seeking in him. To realize my own truth before I could expect to be given it from someone else.

I had not fully forgiven myself for my part in the death of my marriage. Neither had he, and because of that truth, that wound wasn't healed and it showed up. All doubt is self-doubt. His doubts about me, are his doubts about himself. My doubts about him were my doubts about myself.

You can't give pieces of yourself in a relationship. God/The Universe won't allow it for very long before clarification is necessary and the big shake up comes down. You don't need a relationship to fill your needs. You can meet your own needs. A relationship is for sharing love and fulfilling desires.

When someone asks you what you want, don't be afraid to say it. The whole truth of it, not just part of it. Say it and feel good that you said it no matter what happens in the next moment. Above all, make sure you are clear on what you want. When you get into relationship lab, show up fearless, forgiving, honest, gentle, loving and true. Don't come armed for battle or to prove your self worth. Leave your ego at the door. You are the other side of someone else's "Relationship Assignment." You've been paired up in the lab on purpose by God to heal your issue, to help them heal their issue. There can't be healing if there is attack or blame. Be a good lab partner. Come prepared to love and to respond to calls for help with love.

When someone says, "My heart is closed up," believe them. You can ask to hold space and to love it while it opens, or you can give them space to find their way to opening up on their own. If you leave, leave them with your love. It feels much better to leave loving, than hurting, or hating.

When someone says they love your heart, believe them. The truth in that statement is that your presence in their life feels loving, peaceful. You are communicating love and its being recognized. You can love someone enough to let them go. Love truly desires another's happiness, even if they are not a part of their happiness.

Tell the truth, from your heart. Even if it hurts. Even if it might seem to hurt the other person. It hurts less than the alternative. The truth is freeing. Let the other person decide how the truth makes them feel. The purest form of love is pure communication.

You can't fast forward anyone along their path. You can stop and wait and maybe they will catch up and hold your hand and walk along with you, but at some point you might have to start walking again, without them and that is ok.

You always have a choice in a situation. Choose the one that serves YOU best. Don't settle for less than what you really want. Because that is exactly what you will get: less than what you want. That doesn't mean the other person is "less than," or not worthy of your love. It means the person is unable at that moment to be with you in the way that you desire. It means they still have "stuff" to work on internally. Barriers to love to undo for themselves, before they can love fully. Wholly. Let them. If they are meant to walk along with you, God/The Universe will take care of bringing them back when they are able to give as they receive, or will send you your next relationship assignment. Your emotional match.

In the aftermath, look at your part. Find your barrier to love and ask God/The Universe to remove it for your next assignment so you can show up fearless in the moment. Fear is the opposite of Love. God will answer with your emotional equal. Truth be told, I am anxious and excited for the next assignment to grow in. "Anxcitement" is powerful fuel. It's a real turn-on to communicate truth. I dig the heart to heart. The honesty. The connection. The true expression of emotion. It feels so much better than holding it in. I can't wait to sit down at the kitchen table again. That's the kind of fire we all need. *Soul fire.*

A few days later, while in hot yoga, working my, "I love you, but I love myself more," program, I am waiting for the beloved cold lavender towel to fall in my hand, my mind says this. *I want my own version of the fairy-tale.* Two emotionally healthy people, walking along their paths happily together, surrounded by the people they love, supporting each other, sharing a life. The safe place for my heart. A relationship where your truest self expression is accepted and appreciated. Where you feel free, not trapped. Loved never judged. Sanctuary from the rest of the world. Peaceful co existence. Working together in relationship lab, graduating with a Ph.D. in Love. Taking their last breath together singing their songs and their skeletons found 1000's of years later intertwined like they'd been dancing.

Then I heard my heart say, "Be alone." Right then, I knew that I needed some time alone. Really alone. So I took off for a few days to go inside and listen to God speak to my heart. When it all feels very loud and messy, I find it best to get very quiet and take some time alone. Either alone in my house disconnected, or to take a few days actually away, alone. Big shake-ups like divorce, death, break-ups happen and we find ourselves. Our true selves. Grief reveals your heart. It was my time to really know my own heart in a way that was abundantly clear, so I would know exactly how to answer when asked again, "What do you want?" I have high expectations of myself in love and life, that part I know.

Then I heard this: "Be still."

When I hear that, I remember God and I are still hot and heavy. God's got me. The Universe always has my back. I can start walking forward again holding hands with God, paying attention to the signs along the way, keeping my heart open, my head on straight, and feeling solid good. Taking good care of me.

"You, Yourself as much as anyone in the entire Universe deserves your love and affection." -Buddha

There Is No Shortage of Love
The truth is, there is no shortage of Love. Love shows up on your doorstep over and over and at my house it looks like this:

- A little bag of washcloths infused with lavender like the ones you get at the end of hot yoga. Divine.
- Flowers and a note that says, "I am just thinking of you."
- Homemade snickerdoodle cookies and a "green" smoothie to counteract the sugar rush.

- A beautiful flower garden planted in the back yard so you can sit and "be still" in beauty.
- Bags of groceries when you arrive home from the trip where you sent your mom off to Heaven.
- Texts that say, "I picked up your kids and took them to the pool," or, "I took your girls for a mani/pedi."
- Texts that just have hearts, or peace signs, or rainbow emojis. One little second that says, "I care about you, I am thinking of you right now. I love you."
- Casseroles and salads and brownies made with loving hands because you've lost someone, or you are caring for someone who is ill, and your hands are too full to make a meal for your family.
- Messages that say, "I took care of your daughter's t-shirt for the show for you," or "I signed your son up for Scouts, don't worry about a thing, I got you."
- Invitations to beach houses, lake houses and retreats. Places to sit in nature, stare at water and heal.

- Girlfriends bearing bottles of wine and wine soaked peaches.
- Dinners brought to the hospital so you don't have to eat that hospital food.
- Parking vouchers for the hospital parking lot.
- Free valet parking at the hospital.
- Massage gift cards in your mailbox, saying "Please keep taking care of yourself."
- Emails and Facebook posts, cards and letters.
- Hug after hug after hug. In the grocery store, at school, at the coffee shop, everywhere you go.

For most of my life, I'd been looking for someone to take care of me. Once I opened up my heart to people and really opened up my eyes, I realized that there were people taking care of me everywhere. Not just one person, but everyone. All people including strangers. Connected. Love was everywhere. I just hadn't tapped into it.

"If I ever go looking for my heart's desire again, I won't look any further than my own back yard. Because if it isn't there, I never really lost it to begin with." – Frank L. Baum. The Wizard of Oz

The Truth About Love

"Love many things for therein lies the true strength, and whosoever loves much, performs much and can accomplish much, and what is done in love is done well." – Vincent van Gogh

I love to talk about love. Debunk the mystery, unravel mindsets, listen to hearts and tune them up with more love. Help people find the love in their life, and create peace. It's what I do. It's what God asked me to do, therefore I do it with enthusiasm, and it gives me great joy. It's the foundation of my coaching, writing and speaking. Sometimes it takes hitting emotional rock bottom to find the truth of your heart.

These truths I teach in my programs, speak about in workshops, and write about in books and blogs. These truths I know for sure:

- Love is everywhere, in everyone.
- Before you can truly fall in with love another, you must fall in love with yourself.
- The best way to love someone is to let them be exactly who they are, and let them be free. There is no love without freedom and no freedom without love.
- Love doesn't always look like what we expect it to look like – and just because it doesn't look like what we expect it to look like, doesn't mean it isn't love.
- Pure love is pure communication. There is no love without communication. We are here to communicate love to each other, nothing else.
- When two hearts are truly joined they will find a way to be together in their own time.
- You can't make someone share their love with you if they aren't ready.

- You can't make someone accept love when they don't want to be loved.
- Love doesn't attack.
- Love heals.
- Give your best love in the moment. You are only assured this moment.
- It starts with you. The love inside of you.
- You can't be afraid to give your heart. If you hold back your heart in fear, what you will get is another heart held back in fear. Love is handing out your heart over and over again because that's what keeps it open.
- In order to get love you have to give love. Over and over and over.
- Love is unexpected.
- Love leads to love.
- Love doesn't conquer all but it makes it all ok.
- You can't depend on one person to give you all the love you desire.
- You can't give one person all of your love.
- Love asks only that you be happy.
- Love is meant to be shared by everyone.

- There is a force of Love waiting for you, everywhere, in all parts of your life. You just have to tap into it.
- Love yourself the way you want to be loved.
- You can walk your life path with someone you love and while walking, learn how to be a better lover to all.
- To get good love, you have to be a good lover.
- Love always prevails.
- We were created in love. By God. Therefore we are at our core, Love.

Best Love Quotes Ever

"*Love yourself first and everything else falls in line.*"

– Lucille Ball

"*One is loved because one is loved. No reason is needed for loving.*"

– Paulo Coehlo

"*In the end the love you take is equal to the love you make.*"

– The Beatles

"*We are most alive, when we're in love.*"

– John Updike

"*I want a soulmate who can sit me down, shut me up, tell me ten things I don't already know and make me laugh. I don't care what you look like, just turn me on. And if you can do that, I will follow you on bloody stumps through the snow.*"

– Henry Rollins

"Love does not consist in gazing at each other but in looking outward together in the same direction."

— Antoine Saint Exupery

"Love sees not with the eyes but with the mind."

— Shakespeare

"We can do no great things – only small things with great love."

— Mother Teresa

"Where love is, no room is too small."

— Talmud

"When you get down to it, the only purpose grand enough for a human life, not just to love but to persist in love."

— Sue Monk Kidd, The Secret Life of Bees

"You will find as you look back upon your life, that the moments when you have truly lived are the moments when you have done things in the spirit of love."

— Henry Drummond

"Love me without fear, trust me without questioning, need me without demanding, want me without restrictions, accept me without change, desire me without inhibitions, for a love so free will fly away."

– Dick Sutphen

"God crushed my pride and opened my heart to love. All I have to do, the one thing that love requires is that I let others know they are not alone."

– Heaven is For Real

"And now these three remain: Faith, Hope & Love, but the greatest of these is Love."

– Corinthians 13:13

Playlist for a Life You Love

Music heals the soul. Find your soul songs and sing them loud. These are mine.

Beautiful Day – Joshua Radin
Beautiful World – Jim Brickman
Best Day of My Life – American Authors
Best Day of Your Life – Katie Herzig
Bonfire Heart – James Blunt
Boom Clap – Charli XCX
Brave – Sara Bareilles
Calling All Angels – Train
Carry On – Fun
Chances – Five for Fighting
Close Your Eyes – Michael Bublé
Closer to Love – Matt Kearney
Clouds – Zach Sobiech
Cups – Anna Kendrick
Deep Inside of You – Third Eye Blind
Dream Baby Dream – Bruce Springsteen
Edge of Glory – Lady Gaga
Everybody – Ingrid Michaelson
Feel This Moment – Pitbull
Glitter in the Air – Pink

Hair- – Lady Gaga
Here's to Us – Halestorm
How Long Will I Love You – Ellie Goulding
I Lived – One Republic
I Love It – Icona Pop
In Your Shoes – Sara McLachlan
Just Breathe – Pearl Jam
Keep Your Eyes Open – Needtobreathe
Living in the Moment – Jason Mraz
Nothing More – The Alternate Routes
Odds Are – Barenaked Ladies
On Top of the World – Imagine Dragons
Peace – O.A.R.
Roar – Katie Perry
Say – John Mayer
Scare Away the Dark – Passenger
She is Love – Parachute
Simple Love – Alison Krauss
Sing Together – Train
Somebody Like You – Keith Urban
This is Your Sword – Bruce Springsteen
Three Little Birds – Bob Marley
Try – Colbie Calliat
Unconditionally – Katy Perry
What I Got – Sublime

Love Letters to Mom & Dad

MOM

May 22

I sang a little.

"I love you, a bushel and a peck. A bushel and a peck and a hug around the neck."

My mom sang that to us our whole lives. Her dad used to sing it to her. Her dad who said she was the next best thing to Jesus when she was born. So we took a moment and hugged each other around the neck...and told each other, "I love you."

And then I said this:

During the last days with my mom, we sang that song a lot, we hugged and we said, "I love you," over and over.

I love all of you for being here today. You are here because you loved our mom, because our mom loved you. Or you are one of the people that love us or love her grandchildren. How happy are we that Pat, Mom, Grammy, Trishie was loved by so many. That we are loved by so many.

Love is what we all need, especially when we come together this way.

My mom was a collector of beautiful things. She loved to go hunting for antiques, seashells, sea glass, flowers, pillows, signs and sayings, bits and pieces that decorated her life, our lives.

The most beautiful thing she collected, though, was people. She used to wish for the big tight circle of friends like my sister and I have, but the truth was, she was loved by everyone. Everyone she met she called friend and they loved her.

They speak of it to us of how they loved her. "She was so generous, faithful, giving, kind, never a bad word about anyone." "She was like my second mom." "I had a crush on her." She was "unforgettable."

"I will never forget her smile," they say.

"I loved her laugh. She was always laughing."

"I just loved your mom," they say. Every single person.

My mom was a giver. A generous giver of laughter, of smiles, of kindness. Her most generous gifts, though, were life-changing opportunities.

She believed in people, no matter what the circumstances were. She gave many of you your first jobs, opportunities that turned into successful careers and created marriages, and lifelong friendships. More than one person has said, "Everything I have is because of her." That's true for my sister and me too. With my dad, she gave us the opportunity to be stay at home moms, helped us buy those homes, furnish and decorate them. She gave us summers at the beach, winters on the ski slopes and in the Bahamas, all of which gave us plenty of memories to cherish, stories to tell over dinner, or while snuggled up in bed. Memories that make us laugh and smile.

Someone recently asked me if I felt my mom supported me. At first I thought, well, she was a working mom, so she wasn't at all the games when I cheered in high school, she wasn't volunteering in the classroom or at the snack bar. She didn't write me long letters or send care packages when I was away at school, if that's the way you describe support. Her support was far bigger, deeper.

She believed in us, all of us. My dad, my sister and me. And then all the grandkids. She truly believed in our dreams. If we wanted to do it, whatever it was, she supported it because she believed in us. Her support made our dreams come true. Made us believe a little more in ourselves. That is how she showed her love.

From my dad's racing career, my sister's love for animals and talent for fixing up houses, to my entrepreneurial spirit, she believed.

We weren't the only ones.

I imagine that everyone here, touched by her, knows what I am talking about, felt her belief in the possibility of all things. Her belief in you.

My mom is not gone. Her life is not lost. Her life was a huge gain for all of us. I know exactly where she is. She and I talked about God's plan for us a lot this past year. I know she is truly free and peaceful now.

She's with God, but she is not gone.

She will live on in my heart, but more she will live on in all of you, the pieces of her that she planted so that we wouldn't miss her physical presence too much, so that we would know she was still here.

I know she's here when I look in Nancy's "lake" sparkling eyes, and experience her generosity; when I hear my sister's voice and see her expressions; when Charlotte's silly streak shows, and in her gentle strength; when Mitchell hugs and sees the possibility in things; when Ella tells me a story or says something wise; when Jason smiles and lives out his dream; when Alison perseveres with mighty intent; when Darby takes care of and believes in people; when Carley, who is the most like her, gets real stubborn or makes us all belly laugh. I know she's here when I see her love on my dad's heart, a love that spanned more than 50 years, a love that will last forever. A true example of unconditional love.

She loved my dad and always let him be free to be himself and do what made him happy. There wasn't a day that went by that they didn't kiss and say, "I love you." I have perfect memory when I think of how they looked at each other in their loving moments. You could see it, and feel it, and because of it she will never be gone from us.

You will know she's here, too, when you find a tiny piece of seaglass on the beach, in every sea shell, when you see a quilt or an old scale, a folky American flag, a "life is good" t-shirt, or a sign that reminds you to laugh, to believe, to live one day at a time. Or when you remember the way she blessed you with her generosity, a job, an opportunity, some time at the beach, a trip, a long talk, a ride somewhere, her friendship, her care, her time, her faith which changed you a little or a lot, affected your way of life.

Be the best pieces of Pat, our mom, our Grammy.

And she will not be lost.
Shine your light.
Be generous. Share everything you have.
Be a fighter. Fight for your life.

Never Ever Give Up.

Try hard. "'Can't' never did a thing."

Help out.

Dig in the dirt and plant flowers.

Pick up sticks and then drink lemonade.

Look on the bright side.

Believe that "life is good."

Believe in each other.

"Say something nice or don't say anything at all."

Believe in God's plan. Pray.

Find your serenity.

Take it one day at a time.

Don't worry until there is something to worry about.

And then, Keep Calm and Carry On.

Accept people. Let them be free to be themselves and love them unconditionally.

See their light.

Don't be afraid of the dark.

Sit on the porch and tell stories.

Read lots of books.

Go for a ride on the bike.

Keep your toes in the sand.

Don't wait to find your happy place.

Be a silly Grammy.

Jump on the bed, laugh a lot, forget your boob and say you forgot it.

Sing even if you think you can't.

Smile at everyone.

Make people belly laugh.

Be a real friend.

Be grateful for each day if only because you woke up on the right side of the grass.

Be happy.

Dance.

Hug around the neck.

Kiss and say, "I love you."

A bushel and a peck.

Mother's Day – May 11

"The loveliest masterpiece of the heart of God is the love of a mother."
– Therese of Lisieux

A friend sent this to me when I was having my last days with my mom. It echoes in my head, especially in my weepy moments. People have been telling me that today will be difficult, that today will be hard.

The truth is today will be beautiful, because I am a mother, too.

I was blessed with three people who love me like no other, who have my mother's laugh, my mother's smile, her eyes, her knack for storytelling, her silliness, her voice. I will be with my sister, who will make her faces and make me laugh with her expressions, who has her bright spirit, and my nieces who also share her smile and her positive spin on all things. And with my dad whose heart is full of my mom's love, the keeper of her heart.

Today there might be moments of grief. Tears. Missing. There is a person-sized hole in our group. Through it all though I know my mom is here. Her love, her spirit can never disappear. And because of that we can smile and laugh through our tears.

Today will be beautiful, because I am a mother too. I woke up to messages from my children all over my kitchen. How they see me, feel me. Knowing that they fully feel my love is the best gift I could ever imagine.

Today will be beautiful, because of all of you mothers. The ones who have mothered my children when they were in your presence. I am blessed with a community of amazing, loving, generous mothers who wrap their arms around my kids. I've said it before and its still true. The people I love the most are the people who love my children. I love and appreciate you women who have a special bond with each of my children. The Mom #2's. The Extra Mom. We are especially blessed to have you. And those moms who step in and pick up our slack when we really need it, without ever asking. Who just show up. Who are always thinking of others.

Who answer the question, "What can I do," without even asking it.

And because of our friends, who show us *mother love*, every day. Big ways and small ways. By always being "there" for each us. For each other.

Wishing all of you *mother love* today. May your hearts feel full. May you feel all the love that you give out multiplied. You deserve it. Today will be beautiful, because we are loved.

DAD

August 10

"It's going to be a pretty day," he said. It was one of the last things he said to me besides, "I love you."

My dad has been in the trauma unit at the hospital for 12 days. His leg has been amputated, and he's had three surgeries after a motorcycle accident. He is in decline. The comfort care team has been called in. I have been given the "truth talk."

We spent the following day at my dad's side, my sister and I singing the songs from his iPod, a mix of bluegrass, oldies, eagles, Bob Seger, all his favorites. "I love this song!" I must have said 100 times.

We danced around a little, like we did when my sister and I were kids and would play Buddy's 45s in the basement. We laughed and told stories about how we made dad crazy. We cried. We hugged. We hugged his friends that stopped by. We said prayers for peace. We hugged the nurses, and they hugged us back. We told dad about all the people who loved him and how he'd been such a gift to so many people. He helped loads of kids get through high school with a trade and a future. Helped friends fix things, find things, do things they'd never been able to do, get better at stuff, be independent.

Around 7:00, I laid down next to him, pulled out the beautiful ocean blue rosary beads that my friend Maureen gave me for my birthday, and and prayed the rosary out loud. Nurse Jenny walked in and started to cry. I asked her why, and she said, "You're breaking my heart, I've never seen anyone get in bed with someone who was dying.

"I'm not doing it to break your heart," I said. "I am doing it to fill it." and we squeezed hands. After the prayers we sang along with the iPod. I can't remember the song, but I am sure I said, "Oh I LOVE this song," first.

Then Buddy was quiet. He sailed off to dance with my mom, the woman he'd loved almost his whole life.

I like to think of them like this: him saying something only they could hear. Her big smile when she saw him. I am happy for them. All wrapped up together. Free.

August 14

It was a pretty day yesterday. A beautiful day, really. We were surrounded by love, our family, our friends, the people that loved our dad, people that love us. We hugged and hugged and hugged some more. And then I got to talk about my dad. To me, the best part about a funeral, memorial, celebration of life – whatever you want to call it – is hearing some truth about a person's life and how they used their gift for good, how they loved, related, and made people feel. I always hear something that inspires me to be better at being a human. Here is what I said about my dad, Buddy. Take what you want, and be better.

Nichol (my sister) and I were talking the other day about "Showing Up" for people. How it's the best we can give someone, our presence. That's what Buddy, our dad, did.

Every day. He got up, got ready and then showed up for someone. He showed up by helping people, by being a good friend, a good neighbor, by teaching people how to do things, by bringing you something you needed or by making your environment a little bit better. He planted flowers, mowed your grass, spent hours at the driving range perfecting your golf swing, he taught you how to change your oil, rotate your tires, he brought your dog treats, he swung by on his motorcycle for a chat, he explained some complicated chore or fixed your dishwasher, your lawnmower, or your front door for you. He helped people be better. He made things better. He fixed things up.

He always did exactly what he wanted, and what he wanted to do was to do something for you. I know that in some way Buddy showed up for each one of you, somewhere in your life, and that's why you are here.

As a father, grandfather, and a high school teacher, he did something much bigger. He fostered independence and self-reliance, which in turn created personal freedom, strength, confidence, and success in life. Hundreds of his students have valuable skills to offer, have built a better life for themselves, and some have even followed in his footsteps and become teachers who foster the same. His students experienced him much the same way his family did. We were all a little in awe of him because he knew how to do everything, kind of scared because he commanded respect, and wanted his confirmation that we'd done it right. He had high expectations. High, because he could see that you could rise to meet them. He didn't let people off the hook. In fact he expected you to try harder in all things. He was a hard ass, but with a big mushy heart that he kept kind of hidden.

I didn't really see that mushy heart side of him until our mom was dying. I had come to understand the way my dad showed his love. It wasn't soft. It was tough. He was tough. Clint Eastwood tough. When his beloved Pat died three months ago, it broke his heart open. I saw a side of my dad, maybe only my mom knew. He began to express his feelings and love in a way that we had never seen. A wall had come down. I feel blessed that we had the time we had to experience his deeper heart, his tenderness. To see and feel the raw emotion and love for my mom, for us, expressed by the man I'd idolized all my life, was a gift.

I can only be happy that they are together again. I know they are with us. In us, because they created us.

There is a little bit of Buddy inside of all you too. Because he showed up for you. Because he taught you something, how to do something, fix something, to figure things out. He taught you how to show up and help without being asked. He taught you that you can always make something a little bit better, and because of that, you should.

Because of my dad, we can change a tire, build a playground, drive a stick shift.

Because of my dad, we are not afraid of "some assembly required."

We know how to use power tools.

We can jump start a car, with or without jumper cables, mow grass, remove stitches, fix a toilet and maybe one of us might even be able to park a 55 foot yacht.

We know how to take care of a pool, resurface the driveway, cut down trees.

I don't like doing some of that stuff, but I can do it if I have to.

Because of my dad, we like the smell of grease, Marlboros and Brut cologne.

We are totally at home in a garage.

Because of my dad, we can snow ski and water ski. We've searched for seashells, sand dollars and starfish and eaten lobster right out of the ocean in the Bahamas.

We know that "every little thing, is gonna be alright." Especially when you're watching the sunset or doing the electric slide in Treasure Cay.

Because of my dad, we love music. We have a soundtrack to our life. We know all the words to all the songs and we love to dance.

I learned from Buddy that your kids will always mess up your stuff, but you'll love them anyway. That you can wear a thong bathing suit, no matter how old you are. That comfortable is cool, orange is the best color and 13 is lucky.

I learned to push the gas when you needed to get out of a tricky situation and not to be afraid to go fast.

I learned to always kiss and say, 'I love you."

I learned that to be happy you have to do what you want, help others along the way, and love your person deeply.

I learned the best way to love someone is to let them be exactly who they are, and let them feel free. That love doesn't always look like what we expect it to look like and just because it doesn't look like what we expect it to look like doesn't mean it isn't love.

I learned that when two hearts are truly joined they will find a way to be together.

Our dad, Buddy would want you to be happy for him, that he is truly free. Free to be with the woman he loved, free of pain, free to do exactly what he wants. Every day. For Eternity.

Birthday Love Letters

To My Son

He has my whole heart. My unconditional, undying love from the moment I knew he existed, from the moment I laid eyes on his perfect face and in every moment that transpires. His spirit is so bright that it shines through his amazing smile. Being near him makes me feel giddy like I have a buzz. He makes me laugh until I cry and sometimes cry until I laugh. I am pretty sure I will never love a soul the way I love him. Celebrating my son today. Even though he doesn't want to hit this milestone.

It's impossible for me not say a "few" things like...... How much I appreciate your devotion to our family and the way you share your love. Or how much I admire your connection to your friends. The depth, the sensitivity, the loyalty, the faith you have for them, the support you share and the love you give them. I admire your strength, your vulnerability, your core values. The way you speak the truth and open your heart. The path has been a little rocky, painful and unclear at times but through it all you continue to be strong, to be your own person, undaunted, brave, honest, fearless, loving, and true to yourself, your beliefs and desires. You have taught me more about love, life, authenticity and truth than anything or anyone.

I am so proud of the person you are. I am just as proud to be your mother. So I will celebrate your birthday whether you want to or not. The day you were born was one of the greatest days of my life. You made me a mom. You are the best thing I ever did.

Happy Birthday my favorite son. I love you the most. Keep stepping forward confidently and going after it and celebrating the good stuff. With you all the way.

My daughter, Ella

I secretly prayed for her. Every night for a long time. I said "please God, just one more, just one more" I really didn't think it was possible, since we waited so long for Charlotte. But then four years and one day later the AMAZING Ella was born. We've called her the surprise, but really she was there all along just waiting for the right time. Our adorable little fashionista, tiny dancer with the fiercely independent streak, a style all her own, who knows what she wants and is not afraid to ask for it. She loves her family and her friends with a big open heart. She's taught me to be fearless, to be here in the moment (especially with her), to slow down, take our time, not rush, be honest, be open, be confident & strong. She is these things, things I needed to learn to be. She is bold, smart, wise beyond her years. I think she knows more than I do. She really pays attention. All that and a fabulous smile and shining eyes. She has a very bright light! You were right Ella...you are everything I ever wanted to be.

Happy Birthday to our baby! Eight....No way. 8.

Just another perfect gift to dad, Charlotte, Mitchell and I.

These are the days we will remember right Ella?

My daughter, Charlotte

I find it practically impossible to say that Charlotte is 12 today. I keep telling her she is too young to be 12 and there is NO way she can go to middle school in the fall. It's just NOT possible. It took her incredibly long to get here. We waited and waited and prayed and prayed for 7 years. Trying just about everything medically possible to bring her here. Even though in my heart I knew she was coming all along. When she was born in less than a 1/2 hour after a pregnancy on total bed rest (more waiting) she made up for all that Charlotte induced patience. Well...... after the 100 days of crying.

Celebrating my beautiful daughter Charlotte today. The one who dares us to try new things and go new places. Our "trooper" who truly goes with the flow. Our graceful dancer, lover of animals, science enthusiast, generous, caring, sensitive friend, loving sister who knows how to stir up some fun and amazing gift to dad,

Mitchell, Ella and I. Happy Birthday dear sweet Charlotte, Thank you for giving me the best days of my life!

Sister Love

Today is my very first best friend's birthday. My first and favorite side kick. We have our own secret language, we know all the words to all the songs, she laughs the hardest with me, cries the hardest with me, dances when I want to dance and sits still when I need to and carries me when I can't walk by myself. She knows me the only way a sister can, and we are blessed to have each other. My badass, beautiful, incredibly strong but sweetly tender, bright shining sister with the fabulous and unique sense of style, deep caring heart, and positive force. Made of steel but soft as butter on the inside. She'll protect you with a ferocity like you've never known. I love you more than a bushel and a peck. I love you a ton. You are my sunshine!

For My First Love

Today. Today is one of my BEST friends birthdays. I didn't know when we met that we would really become friends forever. We've been friends for 34 years. We met in English class in 9th grade. I had the hugest crush on him. I am sure he caught me staring at him a million times a day. I will never forget the day when he got up to sharpen his pencil and slid a note on my desk.

Swoon.

I adored him. Being around him gave me a buzz. (It still does) He was my first love, my first break up, the boy all the love songs and break up songs were written about from 1980-1983. We've spent hours on the phone talking. We wrote 100's of notes. The greatest thing is that we are still friends after all these years. That first love (after the bad breakups) turned into an amazing and wonderful friendship. It may surprise you to hear that he was in my wedding. I know, unusual. But he's that special to me. He's who I call when I need guy perspective. When no one else understands, when I want to laugh or need to cry it out. He's that way. He's an awesome friend. He gets me. I am blessed with people like this. Happy Birthday to my high school love, my best friend, the big man. Brad, I still adore you. Thanks for still being here. Don't know what I would do without your friendship all these years. lucky girl.

Ex Husband Love

Today is another special day. Without you, there wouldn't be three of the most amazing people in my world. Thanks for being the dad you are to our children. For making sure they all feel loved, for playing littlest pet shops and tea party, for tossing them around in the pool and being a great cannon-baller, for having arms strong enough to carry all the crap to the beach and still hold them out in the big waves. For giving our girls BIG daddy love so that they feel secure and protected. For making them laugh and for riding bikes, playing tennis, shopping at Target and indulging them in their girly stuff. They are ALL SO LUCKY. And blessed to have a dad that loves and participates with them. Wishing you the happiest day today. A birthday filled with peace, joy, love and cake (made by your kids-yum) Happy Birthday Joe Modes You deserve all the love and happiness coming your way.

Acknowledgements

Total and complete gratitude goes first to my children, Mitchell, Charlotte & Ella for learning all the lessons with me and embracing a new way of being. Always dancing, always singing, always in love. Three truly beautiful souls who taught me everything I know about unconditional love.

To Joe for setting me free so I could be me.

To my two angels in heaven. My Mom for always believing in me and reminding me to write with my own pen, the one God gave me.

And my Dad for finally trusting that I knew what to do and for helping me "finish."

To my sister for always having my back, always laughing and lovingly pointing out the obvious.

To my Soul Sister Julie, shells & jewels, there aren't enough words for us.

To my friend Marilyn, who tolerated all of the talks, the "out-there-ness," the trips, the songs, silliness, deep emotion, vulnerability, tears, sobs, fun, laughter and ridiculousness it took to get "exactly where we are supposed to be."

To my Circle of 15, whose love is deep and wide and always in the right hole.

To Gena, who supplied a solid year of love, laughter, mojo and truth.

To the Schmidt's for giving me a place to write and heal, especially when I needed it most.

To Carla for giving me a place to begin again and Robin for building my strength.

To the Rosary group for deepening my faith.

To ALL the ladies in the hood who did the "walkie talkie" and shared their stories, their pain, their joy with me. Especially Kay for starting it with me. (Marion, I know, I owe you a dollar)

To all my people and there are MANY men, women, young and old, who showed up, who loved me and my family through the moments when I felt the least loveable and the most tired. Who took good care of us, helped, hugged, laughed, cooked, smiled and invited us into their lives at times when we felt the most odd and surrounded us with love and gave us beautiful places to heal, especially Ginger.

To Joanne & Sevan for being a shining example of "the second time around."

To Angela, for guiding me across the finish line with full faith in the powerhouse.

To Ginger, my Editor, the voice that made me believe it was all happening.

To 'The Man' whose spirit I love, who sang & danced along a little while. Who opened up the path to my deeper heart and who inspired me to keep doing what I had to do to get my baseball card.

I am the most grateful To God, for tapping me on the shoulder, for firing up my soul, putting all the right people in all the right places, just when I needed them most and showing me how to give from my heart, perfectly.

About the Author

Shelly Young Modes, founder of Start With The Heart, is the go to girl for LOVE seekers of all kinds. Currently on tour teaching others how to "Fall in Love with Your Life." She's an author, speaker, entrepreneur, and mother to three fascinating souls. Her soul mission is to spread love, inspire faith, and create healing & peace through human connection. The bottom line, to help the world feel "Solid Good." You can find her online at www.shellymodes.com or hugging it out with people all over town.

About Difference Press

Built for aspiring authors who are looking to share transformative ideas with others throughout the world, Difference Press offers life coaches, healing professionals, and other non-fiction authors a comprehensive solution to get their book published without breaking the bank or taking years. A boutique-style alternative to self-publishing, Difference Press boasts a fair and easy-to-understand profit structure, low-priced author copies, and author-friendly contract terms.

Tackling the technical end of publishing

The comprehensive publishing services offered by Difference Press mean that your book will be designed by an experienced graphic artist, available in printed, hard copy format, and coded for all eBook readers, including the Kindle, iPad, Nook, and more. We handle all of the technical aspects of your book creation so you can spend time focusing on your business.

Over 20 years of experience nurturing books that make a difference

Founder Dr. Angela Lauria has been bringing the literary ventures of authors and personal coaches to life since 1994. You can learn more about Dr. Lauria's innovative approach to book creation or take advantage of a variety of free writing resources at www.TheAuthorIncubator.com

Your Delicious Book

If you're like many authors, you have wanted to write a book for a long time, maybe you have even started a book … or two… or three … but somehow, as hard as you have tried to make your book a priority other things keep getting in the way. Some authors have fears about their writing abilities or whether or not what they have to say is important enough. For others, the challenge is making the time to write their books or having the accountability to see it through to the end. It's not just finding the time and confidence to write that is an obstacle, the logistics of finding an editor, hiring an experienced designer, and figuring out all the technicalities of publishing stops many authors-in-transformation.

For more information on how to participate in our next Your Delicious Book program visit www.TheAuthorIncubator.com/delicious.

Other Books by Difference Press

Why Smart People Do Stupid Things by Dr. Frank Stass

Radical Abundance: A Journey from Not Enough to Plenty by Christy Lambert

Surviving 30: Waking Up to Your True Self Through Your Saturn Return by Karen Hawkwood

Choosing Delight: True Life Stories of Quitting a Soul-Sucking Job and Doing What You Love for a Living by Leyla Day

Own It: Powerful Speaking For Powerful Women by Tricia Karp

Personal Alchemy: The Missing Ingredient For Law Of Attraction Success by Michelle Martin Dobbins

Married To A Vegan: Is It For Better Or For Worse When A Spouse Embraces Healthy Living And A Plant-Based Low-Fat Diet by Caren Albers

Speak Up For Your Business: Presentation Secrets for Entrepreneurs Ready to Tell, Sell, and Compel by Michelle Mazur Ph.D.

The Crowdfunding Book: A How-to Book for Entrepreneurs, Writers, and Inventors by Patty Lennon

Thank You

For my readers, a little thank you gift, visit the website *shellymodes.com* for a free download: "Raise Your Lovability" Transformation Video.

I am also available as a speaker on topics such as "Divorce Rehab"
"Someone Stole Your Perfect"
"Finding Your Sweet Spot"
"Manifesting Mojo"
"Fall in Love with Your Life"

Connect with me on Facebook at Start With The Heart or by email *shellymodes@gmail.com*.

Made in the USA
Middletown, DE
18 December 2014